THE LAST OF THE COCKLESHELL HEROES

THE LAST OF THE COCKLESHELL HEROES

A WORLD WAR TWO MEMOIR

by WILLIAM SPARKS
DSM
with
MICHAEL MUNN

LEO COOPER
LONDON

First published in Great Britain in 1992 by
LEO COOPER
190 Shaftesbury Avenue, London WC2H 8JL
an imprint of
Pen & Sword Books Ltd.,
47 Church Street, Barnsley, S. Yorks S70 2AS

A CIP catalogue record for this book is available
from the British Library

ISBN O 85052 297 8

Typeset by Yorkshire Web, Barnsley, South Yorkshire
in Plantin Roman 10 point

Printed in Great Britain by The Redwood Press Limited,
Melksham, Wiltshire.

CONTENTS

CHAPTER 1   *1*

CHAPTER 2   *23*

CHAPTER 3   *45*

CHAPTER 4   *57*

CHAPTER 5   *74*

CHAPTER 6   *88*

CHAPTER 7   *101*

CHAPTER 8   *117*

CHAPTER 9   *133*

CHAPTER 10   *141*

INDEX   *149*

With Love
to
Irene

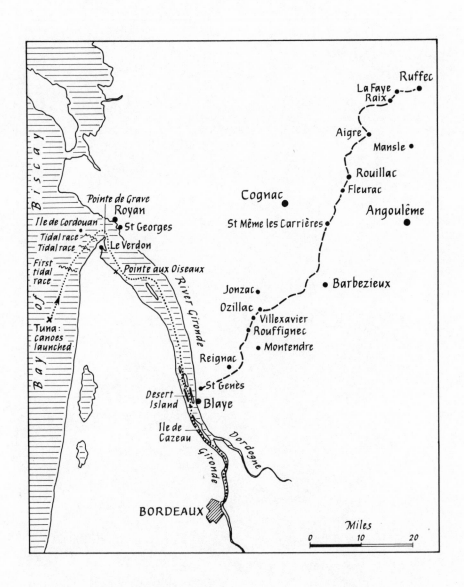

1

'THERE'S NO DOUBT ABOUT IT,' said the doctor, 'The bronchitis you suffer each winter is due to your war service.'

This was not something that came as a bolt out of the blue to me really. Ever since the day I fell into the sea while stationed in Iceland during the war and caught bronchial pneumonia, I had gradually begun to suffer. But I wasn't bitter at all. I had played my part in the war. I was one of the so-called Cockleshell Heroes and had been awarded the Distinguished Service Medal for my part in Operation Frankton. My medal had become my most treasured possession, presented to me personally by King George VI.

'What do I do now?' I asked the doctor.

'Well, you can apply for a war disability pension, and you may have to consider early retirement.'

I made my claim and underwent investigation to ascertain that my disability was due to war service. I was suitably graded and then informed that, whilst responsibility by the Military was accepted, my grade did not qualify me for a pension.

In due course, I retired. My wife, Rene, and I dreamed of buying a house in the country, and we set our hearts on a bungalow in Sussex. We placed a deposit, having decided we could afford it if we handled our affairs carefully, and moved in. I had a reasonable pension from my employers, London Transport, for whom I'd been a bus driver, a bus inspector and finally a garage inspector, and I had my state pension. We could just manage.

Then came a terrible blow. The Government decided to reduce my state pension by £1,000 a year. My wife and I were thunderstruck at the thought that we could lose our home. We racked our brains trying to see how we could cope on £1,000 less a year. Finally we realized that we would have to sell something to make up the difference.

With great reluctance, I put a call through to Sotheby's and asked them if they would auction my most prized possession — my medal.

Before long, newspapers were carrying the story that the last of the

Cockleshell Heroes was compelled to sell his medal. After that, hundreds of letters of support poured in. Most said how outraged they were that my pension should have been cut. One young man telephoned me in tears, saying how disgusted he was with the way I was being treated, and he offered to give me £10 a week out of his own wages. Close to tears myself, I declined his kind offer.

I had another offer by telephone from a gentleman living abroad who offered to send me £12,000 providing that I did not sell the medal. It was generous of him, but I could not accept charity.

The day of the auction arrived and Rene and I boarded the train for London. And as we sped along I recalled that years earlier I had taken another train ride to London, at a time when the world was at war.

The train rumbled on through the night. Looking out into the darkness of the countryside, I could not see so much as a single twinkling light as England was plunged into total blackout. If Hitler's Luftwaffe were in the skies tonight, I saw no sign of them, nor heard them above the clatter of the train. Except for the inky blackness it was almost as though, for a brief while, England was at peace, banishing all thoughts of war for myself and two of my shipmates from the *Renown* — one a Marine and the other a stoker and, like myself, a Cockney.

We had been cooped up on the train since the previous day when we'd boarded at Edinburgh; the *Renown* and the long search for the *Bismarck* were left far behind. Ahead lay fourteen wonderful days' leave in London. It was a long time since I'd been home; a long time since I'd seen Dad.

Dear old Dad. I thought he was going to kill me the day I joined the Royal Marines. I had originally decided, at the outbreak of war, to follow Dad's footsteps; he'd been a stoker in the Royal Navy at the time I was born on 5 September, 1922 — the country was then still reeling from the General Strike. In 1939, when the storm clouds were gathering over Europe, I took myself off to the local recruitment office to join the Royal Navy. However, a sergeant there convinced me I was too intelligent a lad for the Royal Navy. He produced brochures featuring exciting photographs of smart young Marines wearing their 'lion tamer' tunics and gleaming white helmets, standing beneath palm trees on some exotic island, surrounded by beautiful girls in grass skirts. He convinced me; this was the life for me.

I was led into another room for a medical examination. Passed fit in every respect, I was handed a Bible, sworn in and given half a crown.

'You are now a Royal Marine recruit, lad,' beamed the sergeant. 'Now you go on home and wait for your call up.'

Proud as a peacock, I marched smartly home; but my steps faltered as I was suddenly struck by the thought of confessing to Dad that I had joined the Marines without consulting him.

I waited with apprehension for Dad to return home from work that evening. He came in through the door and, summoning up all my courage, rather haltingly, I told him what I had done.

'*What?*' he exploded. 'You stupid little so-and-so, I ought to knock you from here to next year . . .' And he continued in that vein for a while until a thought occurred to him. He quietened down and, still furious, said, 'You're still only seventeen. When the papers come through I'll refuse to sign them. That'll put a stop to all this nonsense.'

I didn't have the courage to tell him that his signature would not be required.

And so in 1939, as a young Marine recruit, I had caught the train from Charing Cross to attend training camp in Deal. Now I was returning three years later as a full Marine who had seen action in the Mediterranean. But I still hadn't seen a single girl in a grass skirt.

Morning came as we hit the outskirts of London. Our excitement rose and we talked of the days ahead, of the families we'd not seen for so long, of the reprieve from battle, and the simple thought of how lucky we were to be home. Then we hit North London and our joy was diminished by the view from our carriage of a city that had endured nightly punishment. Everywhere were piles of rubble that had been houses, shops, factories, theatres, even churches. Slowly pulling into King's Cross station, we passed railmen filling in bomb craters and repairing buckled track.

The train came to a juddering halt. We cheered up, eager to get home, and climbed out onto the platform. At the ticket barrier, reunited sweethearts kissed and hugged and returning sons embraced their parents. For others, about to board the train, it was a moment of heartbreak and farewell.

Outside the station we found ourselves in the middle of a war-torn city. Many buildings were pockmarked or blackened by fire, and the roads were peppered with craters. Facing the enemy's bombs and bullets was an everyday occurrence for me and my shipmates, but at least we had the comfort of being able to fire back. All our civilians could do was take shelter and hope for the best. Yet even amid this destruction, people were going about their daily business; shops were open, the buses and tubes were running — an abnormal existence had been turned into normality. Clearing the rubble and filling in the craters had just become part of the way of life. To servicemen like ourselves returning from combat zones, this was a revelation. These were non-combatants standing up to combat, and their spirit was unbroken. We felt very proud of them at that moment.

'Well, I'm off to Finsbury Park,' I told my two shipmates. 'We'll meet in two weeks.'

'If we're still sober and standing,' they joked.

I knew *I'd* still be standing, for although I enjoyed a drop of beer I never drank heavily. I had known too much misery in my childhood when Mum and Dad got regularly drunk every Saturday. Not that I blamed them because in those days if you were lucky enough to have a job — and both my parents did eventually find jobs — it was the way of things to join the throng of Saturday night drinkers. But after the drinking came the arguments and the fights. As they drunkenly rolled home the insults flew, followed by the fists. Each gave as good as they got. I was only about two or three, but I can remember screaming and begging them to stop.

One of their drunken brawls very nearly resulted in our house burning down. That night the paraffin lamp — our only form of lighting, apart from candles — was knocked over in the foray, and the spilled paraffin burst into flames. Before the fire got out of control, Mum and Dad ceased hostilities and joined forces to put out the fire. But this didn't deter them from future Saturday night drink-and-fight sessions.

So, no, I didn't expect to be too legless to meet up with my shipmates again in a fortnight. We said our goodbyes and I found the appropriate bus stop. Dad had been bombed out of our previous home and now lived in Finsbury Park. Fortunately I was familiar with that area. He'd also remarried and I had yet to meet my step-mum.

The bus arrived and I climbed aboard, astonished to find that the conductor was a female. I had forgotten that women had taken on many jobs usually done by men.

'Come on, luv, hold very tightly,' she said cheerfully. She rang the bell and the bus shunted forwards. I fell into a seat.

'Finsbury Park, please,' I said holding out my fare money.

'Home on leave?' she asked.

'Yes.'

'You keep your money, luv,' she said with a warm smile.

'But we all have to pay our way,' I insisted.

'I wouldn't hear of it, a man like you fighting to keep this country free,' she said. 'You've done more than enough to pay for a single bus fare.' No matter how much I tried to pay, she insisted my money was 'no good here'.

With more warm smiles, she set me off at my stop and I went off in search of Fonthill Road. I had written instructions on how to find Dad's address so it wasn't long before I was in the right street. But I was apprehensive in case I'd got the address wrong. I came to the house — or what I hoped was the house. I rapped on the door and waited. After a few anxious moments, the door was opened by a woman. I didn't know her from Eve.

'Does Mr Sparks live here?' I asked nervously. 'I'm his son, Bill.'

She looked at me quizzically. 'Sparks?' she mused. 'No, there's no Mr Sparks here.'

My heart sank. 'Well, I'm sorry to bother you,' I said.

'Like I said, he's not here.' A mischievous smile spread over her face as she added, 'Because he's still at work.'

'You mean, this is the right address?'

'Yes,' she said. 'Welcome home, Bill!' She threw her arms around me then led me inside. 'I'm sorry to have teased you,' she said. 'Your Dad says I've got a wicked sense of humour. And you looked so worried, I couldn't resist playing a little joke.'

I was glad he had married a woman with a sense of humour. How much life had changed for him — for us all — since the General Strike of 1926. When I struggled into the world, Dad was earning a pittance as a stoker in the Royal Navy. We lived in a tiny cramped two-up, two-down in the East End. Upstairs lived Aunt Mary and her four children. We occupied the downstairs rooms where the floorboards were rotten, often giving way.

We couldn't afford the paraffin for the lighting so we had to use candles. Because coal was beyond our means we had to burn whatever timber could be scrounged until, during a particularly cold spell, the bannisters finally went up in smoke. After that we stayed warm by going to bed. Our greatest luxury was the naval blanket we had to cover ourselves.

I was six months old when Dad left the Royal Navy. Like thousands of other demobbed servicemen, he joined the swarming ranks of the unemployed. My mother had to become the breadwinner, working in a tobacco factory, enabling us to afford margarine for our bread and paraffin for the lamps. Then, when I was two, Dad found work in a factory, and the extra money coming in bought a few more luxuries — and a lot of misery each Saturday night. Eventually my parents separated, and with my sister and brother, both younger than me, I moved to a new house with Dad.

Since then he had raised us on his own, so I was especially close to him; and now that I was home on leave I couldn't wait to see him. Finally, early that evening, I heard him step through the front door.

'Bill!' He clasped me by the shoulders and hugged me. 'This is a cause for celebration,' he beamed. 'How about a drink at the local first?'

I wasn't averse to one or two drinks; I hadn't tasted a decent drop of beer since leaving London, so off we went to the local.

Later that evening Dad threw a fine party for me, inviting relatives and friends who insisted I relate my experiences in action. I was more interested in hearing about how everybody coped with the bombings. That night I heard stories of real courage and determination in the face of terror and violence, and to me it seemed their experiences made my own pale into insignificance.

'Right, enough of the blitz,' they said. 'Now we want to hear what you've been up to.'

I gave in and proceeded to relate the events of the previous weeks in the Mediterranean.

The lighter pulled away from the Scapa Flow jetty. On deck stood Marines and sailors complete with kitbags, all waiting to join their assigned ships. I was among them. The lighter slowly circled the harbour, depositing the men at their destroyers, cruisers and battleships. Finally, those of us who remained saw the *Renown*.

As we drew closer to the beautiful grey lines of our battlecruiser, I stared in awe at the hugh 15in gun turrets that dominated her. She bristled with guns; surely, I thought, nothing could withstand an onslaught delivered by this ship. I was fit to burst with pride and confidence.

We drew in alongside and a crane from the ship lowered a line to hoist our kitbags aboard. The admiral's gangway, a wooden stairway weighing some two or three tons, was put over and secured. We scrambled across it and stepped onto the quarterdeck of the *Renown*. As was the naval tradition, out of respect for Admiral Nelson, when we reached the top we turned to face aft and saluted.

We were escorted below decks to the Marine office where we were greeted by the detachment sergeant major. He lectured us sternly about how we were expected to behave on board, especially since there were 1,100 sailors, for there was strong competition between the two services. He introduced us to our home on the mess deck and showed us our allotted messes; mine was 45 Mess, a number that, like our regimental numbers, was never to be forgotten. Spaces were allocated to us for slinging our hammocks. The older hands watched in expected amusement as we clambered up into our hammocks, but we disappointed them as not one of us fell out. I had never actually spent a night in a hammock before; but we had travelled far and so I never slept better than that night.

The morning arrived with a blast of reveille, played by the Marine bugler. We lashed and stowed our hammocks and mustered outside the Marine office to meet the Commanding Officer, a captain. He gave us the usual pep talk about not letting the Corps down, and then we were shown over as much of the ship as would affect us. Finally we were allocated our action stations. I had a yearning to be part of the 15in gun crew and was disappointed to find myself assigned as a member of the 4.5in dual gun crew.

As the days wore on and the novelty of being on a big ship wore off, we grew eager to see some action. As other ships passed, heading out to sea, their crews called out to us, jeering:

'What's the matter; don't you blokes know your way past the boom?' Or: 'Got your anchor stuck to the bottom?'

Then one day we were ordered to 'provision ship'. The stores were to be loaded with meat, ammunition, everything we were liable to need at sea. The 'buzz' of speculation ran round the ship. Obviously we were about to leave harbour, but where were we going? One seaman swore, 'Got it straight from the Admiral himself; we're going to Freetown.'

Stores completed, our picket boats were hoisted aboard. Excitement ran through the entire ship, and we were closed in at action stations. The giant anchor was hoisted. The screws started turning. Then we were on the move.

The great bows of our battlecruiser swept through the boom of Scapa Flow and we turned south towards the Irish Sea. The sea was choppy and before long we were rolling in a strong Atlantic swell. I'd heard a great deal about sea-sickness, but even in this heavy sea I was convinced it would never strike me.

We were accompanied by our faithful watch-dog destroyers, scuttling about, listening for any sign of the feared U-boats, as we steamed steadily southward. The bows dipped deep into the swell and rose again like a majestic sea beast. Down went the bows once more, and up again. I felt a thickness in my throat and remembered what we'd had for dinner that day. Again the bows rose slowly, very slowly, and then fell on an even keel again. My stomach rolled with the ship. I could taste my dinner at the back of my ever thickening throat. My nostrils were filled with the smell of shale oil from the guns. I could hold on no longer, and heaved violently, again and again. My head felt fit to burst, my eyes filled with water and my stomach contracted with each roll of the swell. Since that day I have been in far rougher waters, but there was never anything to compare with that first feeling of sea-sickness.

Throughout the night, all action stations had to stand to, manning positions in case of any sudden attack out of the dark. Came the dawn of our first morning at sea. I was relieved not to have seen any action that night, if for no other reason than the fact that I felt so ill that I figured I would have been more a liability than an asset.

Action stations over, we bade farewell to our watch-dogs. The destroyers turned about to return to port while we sped on alone. As the next few days passed, so did my *mal de mer* and I felt ready to do my part in the defence of the ship.

After a few days we steamed into sight of the Rock of Gibraltar. So much for the buzz that we were heading for Freetown. We slackened speed and the *Renown* slowly and majestically entered the bay outside Gibraltar, ready to enter harbour. All hands were mustered on the upper deck, as is the custom upon entering harbour, and as we passed each ship at anchor the bugle sounded and our salute was given, to be returned by the anchored ships.

We moored alongside the jetty and made fast. Then we learned we were to have the honour of being the flagship of Admiral Sir James Somerville, Commander-in-Chief in the western Med. The Admiral's flag was hoisted and he was piped aboard. He had the reputation of being a bulldog who was only happy at sea, so no time was lost in re-provisioning the ship. And we once more swept out to sea.

Leaving Gibraltar harbour was something of a cat-and-mouse game as there were enemy agents in Spain who watched our every move. We hoped to baffle them each time we left harbour. If we intended to go east, we steamed westward until nightfall, and then slipped back through the Strait under cover of darkness.

Our mission on this occasion was to patrol the Atlantic and flush out enemy raiders. It also gave us the opportunity to brush up our gunnery practice, which was about all we did accomplish that time out since we didn't meet a single enemy ship.

We returned to harbour at Gibraltar and were just tying up at our jetty when over the ship's Tannoy came, 'Air raid warning red. Air raid warning red.'

A bugler sounded the alert and the ship was suddenly alive with men scurrying to action stations. Part of my job was to defend the ship against aircraft. Swiftly we closed up around the gun. Once we were in the turret we could see nothing. We strained like dogs on a leash, ready and eager to go into action for the first time. With the 4.5in shell in the fusing machine, we awaited further instructions from our transmitting station.

'Aircraft in sight, commence, commence, commence,' came the order. The first shell was slipped into the breech of the gun. Seconds later there was a mighty roar and the gun pumped back on the recoil. Its shell soared into the sky, exploding and scattering shrapnel among the bandits, followed by twenty further shells that filled the sky with explosions. The bandits turned tail before they even had a chance to unleash their own deadly cargo. The first round was to us.

Our next mission, along with other ships of the fleet, was to meet a large convoy and escort it towards Cape Town. Accompanying us was the aircraft carrier *Ark Royal*. Together we were known as 'the Terrible Twins'. We joined up with the convoy going south. From time to time U-boats came snooping around but our little destroyers dashed about like terriers, forcing them to submerge and keeping them at bay until we were out of range.

A spotting plane from the *Ark Royal*, which had circled the convoy during the hours of daylight, returned to report that two enemy armed merchant ships were nearby. We immediately handed the convoy over to other ships of the fleet and, accompanied by two destroyers, headed off in the direction of the reported enemy ships.

We steamed for about two hours before spotting smoke from a ship's funnel on the horizon. We sped towards the ship and stopped. The enemy ship was ordered to heave to.

'This is a neutral ship,' her captain responded. 'You must allow us to proceed.'

Our Admiral was not convinced. 'Heave to,' he ordered, 'or we will open fire.'

The ship had no alternative but to obey. A cutter was lowered with a boarding party of Marines and sailors who found a prize crew of German Marines. They were brought aboard for questioning, all except the captain who refused to leave his ship and warned that explosive charges were due to go off at any moment.

Our boarding party was immediately withdrawn and we began to steam away. A few minutes later there were several explosions from within the bowels of the vessel. Fires sprang up from stem to stern. We watched as the ship began to slide beneath the sea's surface, taking her captain with her.

Her sister ship was not far away and we had no trouble finding her. We figured that the first ship had managed to contact her, warning her of her own fate, because the crew gave up without any argument. Only the captain defiantly remained; he intended to go down with his ship, he informed us.

This time we had no time to waste, waiting to see if he was bluffing or if explosives had indeed been set. We commenced firing with our secondary armament. The guns blazed and the ship was torn apart by the onslaught. Fires raged throughout her as we steamed away, allowing another German captain to go down with his ship.

We returned to the convoy, relying on the 'eyes' of the *Ark Royal* to search for further enemy ships. It was finally decided that the convoy was safe enough to continue without us and we returned to Gibraltar.

On land that night I was included in a 'fisting party', with the task of grabbing drunken sailors returning from shore leave and putting them in the cells for the night. This wasn't a popular job as we had all become pretty good friends by then. But we carried out our orders with good humour — only occasionally did a drunken sailor become violent, forcing us to restrain him any way we could.

Standing on 'fisting' detail, I heard a disastrously tuneless version of 'Nellie Dean' coming from the shore and turned to see a matelot friend of mine making his unsteady way back towards the ship. I warned him to pipe down but he went on singing at the top of his voice. 'There's an old mill by the stream, Nellieeee Deeeeaaan . . . .'

It was too late. His wailing brought the officer of the watch out.

'Belay that row,' he ordered.

'Join in with me,' said the sailor. 'Nellie Dean . . . sweeeet Nellieeee Deeeeaaan.'

'Right,' said the officer, 'throw him in the brig.'

I took him by the arms and led him below and into a cell, slammed the door shut and stood guard outside. After a while he began to plead with me through the ventilation hole in the door. 'Bill, give us a cigarette. I haven't got any of my own. Be a mate, Bill.'

I lit a cigarette and pushed it far enough into the ventilation hole so he could draw on it without taking it into the cell. He finished the cigarette and a short while later the officer of the watch came down. His nose seemed to twitch. 'Have you been smoking?' he asked.

'Me, sir? No, sir.'

He began inspecting all the cells, and when he came to the cell which my friend occupied he noticed a nicotine stain around the ventilation hole. I was sure I was about to be charged for smoking while on guard.

The officer pondered for a moment or two, then said, 'I suggest you use a fire extinguisher if you see any more smoke coming from that cell.'

'Yes, sir,' I said, and breathed a sigh of relief.

Our next trip to sea was to accompany a convoy of merchant ships on their way to Malta. These convoys were often attacked by the Italian Air Force who bombed from very high altitudes, usually missing their targets altogether. They really were not much of a threat and could be kept at bay with anti-aircraft fire. But lately the Luftwaffe had been giving the Italians a helping hand. The German was a different pilot altogether. He would come in at all altitudes, and was far more accurate with his bombing.

Two days passed peacefully and we began to think that the stories we had heard had been exaggerated. Nevertheless, we were closed up around our guns continually.

The third day dawned. It was just as daylight began to spread that the alarm sounded. High above us came the first wave of Italian aircraft. The sea exploded all around us. If they had had the courage to come in lower, they would have had better results. Only a few of their bombs made contact with the merchant ships and casualties were at a minimum. We fired back, pumping shells into the sky, scattering the planes and sending them home.

But it wasn't over. A second wave of enemy aircraft fell out of the sky; and these were German bombers. They buzzed around the convoy like mosquitoes, this way and that, coming at us from every direction, at every altitude. They dive-bombed, and opened up with their machine guns. A number of merchant ships were directly hit. Our gallant little destroyers dashed to and fro, picking up survivors.

Our gun turret burned as we fired round after round at the buzzing Luftwaffe. The attacks continued through the day, but as dusk settled the Germans decided to head for home. We took count of our losses. We'd lost several merchant ships; some were still burning. The destroyers finished collecting the remaining survivors. But still the Luftwaffe had failed, for the bulk of the convoy was intact. Malta would receive its much needed supplies. We handed the convoy over to the eastern Med fleet and turned home for Gibraltar.

After a few day's rest, we were sent out to accompany another convoy to Malta. This time we encountered particularly weak bombing raids and sailed virtually unmolested almost to Sardinia. This made Admiral Somerville suspicious, and he sent out a scouting plane. It returned to report that between us and Malta waited the Italian fleet. Admiral Somerville liked nothing more than a good sea battle and, accompanied by another battleship, a heavy cruiser and several destroyers, we steamed full speed ahead to meet the enemy fleet. It didn't bother him that they outnumbered us three to one.

We saw their smoke on the horizon and closed in on them. The Admiral ordered the 15in guns to open fire. They boomed out their savage challenge and we saw the huge splashes as our shells landed close to the first of their cruisers. The Italian fleet suddenly increased their speed, but instead of closing with us to make a battle of it, they were running away, firing hopelessly as they went. We gave chase, firing our guns and scoring several hits on them while they made only one hit on one of our cruisers. The Admiral proclaimed it an outstanding success.

News of our victory over the Italian fleet had reached Gibraltar by the time we returned, and as we led the fleet into harbour we were greeted by a pipe band and tumultuous cheering from the soldiers garrisoned at the Rock.

A few days later we escorted another convoy towards Malta — a particularly large convoy this time, so we knew we could expect trouble. After two days we met the usual wave of Italian aircraft, bombing from high altitudes and causing little damage. We fired our 4.5 shells at them and aircraft from the *Ark Royal* took to the skies to repel them.

The Italians proved no match for our pilots but there were some casualties on our side. One of our pilots was Admiral Somerville's nephew. The Admiral stood on the bridge and watched helplessly as his nephew was shot down.

Under cover of night the enemy tried another ruse, sending in torpedo boats. But the efficiency of our destroyers foiled them and they were unable to break through our destroyer screen. Daylight broke and with it came another, more ferocious, air attack. Bombs literally rained down on the convoy and we hit back with everything we had. The turrets of our 4.5 guns virtually glowed red hot.

Then came a terrible accident. A raider was diving to machine-gun us, so one of our 4.5 turrets swung round to follow it, firing as it turned. It swung too far and too low, blasting the neighbouring turret. Several of the gun crew were killed.

Having survived the onslaught in which we lost a number of ships, the convoy was eventually delivered to Malta, and we turned for home, our hearts heavy with the loss of some of our comrades. Outside the danger zone we paused to bury our dead. The ship's crew that could be spared gathered on the quarterdeck. The Admiral said some fitting words and the last post was sounded. The bodies of our fallen comrades quietly slipped over the side into the watery depths. Hardened as we all were to battle and to death, not a man among us failed to shed tears.

There followed a brief spell in harbour, giving us time to compose ourselves. Then once again we put to sea. Weighing anchor, we headed west, suggesting that we would turn, to fool any spies, and that the following dawn we would find the sun rising over our bows.

But to our surprise the sun came up over the stern. We were still steaming westward, into the Atlantic.

After a few days we were steaming northwards, accompanied by the *Ark Royal*, and the rumours began. 'Heard it straight from the Admiral himself, we're going home,' was the common buzz. Surely not, I thought; not with the Admiral still on board.

The ship's Tannoy crackled and we heard the commander's voice. 'The German battleship, *Bismarck*, is on the loose and is probably heading south for the Atlantic. However, she will probably soon be sunk since the *Hood* (the largest battlecruiser in the world) and the *Prince of Wales* are on her tail. That is all.'

So now we knew we weren't going home; we were there just in case the *Bismarck* should slip through. Daily we were kept up to date by our commander. 'The *Bismarck* has still not been brought to action although the *Hood* and the *Prince of Wales* are closing in on her and action is inevitable.'

We were by now cruising off the coast of France, west of Brest, just in case the *Bismarck* tried to make her way to port. The weather was atrocious and the seas very heavy. Pilots from the *Ark Royal* flew patrols in search of the *Bismarck*. How they managed to get the aircraft off the rolling deck of the carrier I can't say; perhaps just sheer courage and skill.

Darkness fell but there was no news of any sea action. We knew now that the *Bismarck* was heading for Brest, so it was down to us to see that she did not escape. The whole crew were eager to get a crack at her. What we didn't realize was what a formidable vessel she was. Even the Admiralty had underestimated her.

Slowly we cruised up and down. We were already closed up at action stations. At last the alarm rattles sounded. Out of the mist came a ship, looming up into our sights. Our 15in guns trained on the target; we couldn't possibly miss at this range. The guns were loaded. The interceptors were closed. All that remained was for the director to pull his trigger and the *Bismarck* would be blown out of the water.

We waited for the loud explosion that would proclaim the *Bismarck* was no more. But it never came. At the last moment, the target ship gave the recognition signal. It was one of our own cruisers.

That night the *Renown* pitched and rolled in the heavy seas. It seemed an eternity before daylight broke. The Tannoy began to crackle and the commander's voice broke the eerie silence that had fallen upon us throughout the night.

'I have to report to you,' he said sombrely, 'that the *Hood* and the *Prince of Wales* engaged the *Bismarck* early this morning and, after a short action, the *Hood* received a hit in her magazine. The result is that the *Hood* was lost. The *Prince of Wales* has lost contact with the *Bismarck*, so if she has managed to get this far, it is now up to us to get her.'

Patrols were still being sent constantly from the *Ark Royal*. The thick clouds were so low that the pilots were having to skim the water to see anything at all, let alone sight a ship. Our fear was that the *Bismarck* had escaped and would live to fight another day. We wanted revenge for the loss of the *Hood*.

Then came the news: one of the *Ark*'s pilots had sighted the *Bismarck*. The activity on board the cruiser was near to panic; they couldn't afford to lose sight of her. Swordfish aircraft were loaded with torpedoes, weighing them down, making it even more perilous for the pilots to take off from the heaving decks. As each plane left the deck, it dropped suddenly and, struggling, rose to continue on towards the target.

The *Bismarck* suddenly found herself besieged by our planes. They loosed their torpedoes. Several explosions went up from the sides of the ship as direct hits were made. But she kept going. It seemed nothing could sink her — and still her guns were blazing. Then she began to steam around in a circle and we realized her steering gear had been damaged. This allowed one of our cruisers to catch up and administer a torpedo attack, quickly followed by further attacks from our destroyers. Explosions ripped through the *Bismarck* until eventually she came to a dead stop. Still her guns roared back as one of our heavy ships, the *Rodney*, steamed within easy range of her and began pumping her enormous 16in shells into the stricken vessel.

Mortally wounded, the *Bismarck* fired back with all she had. And then she began to sink. As she slipped below the surface, a huge cloud of steam rose up, the waters boiling. The *Hood* had been avenged and the seas had been cleared of a great menace to Allied shipping. But it had taken a large portion of the British fleet to accomplish the destruction of just one enemy ship. I wondered what would have happened had the *Bismarck* been accompanied by her sister ship, the *Tirpitz*.

15

We turned once again towards Gibraltar for a few days' respite and to await the next call of duty. A day or two later the battleship HMS *Barham* arrived at the Rock. Entering the harbour, she tied up at the jetty just in front of us. I thought it curious that she should tie up ahead of the Admiral's ship.

The following morning the ship's company was summoned to clear decks and muster on the quarterdeck, as the Admiral wished to address us. Of course, the buzz began to circulate like wildfire. We were due for a refit and we guessed that this was it. But where would we go? There were those who insisted, 'Heard it straight from the Admiral himself — Freetown.'

Admiral Somerville arrived on the quarterdeck, looking unusually solemn as he began his address. 'The *Renown* is due for a refit with more modern equipment. As you know, I'm very fond of the *Renown*. Well, I can't say where the refit will take place — I can't say because I don't know myself. But I want to thank you all for the way you have served your country, and this ship, and I wish you all good hunting in the future.'

That evening all the Admiral's equipment and papers were transferred to HMS *Barham* and we said farewell to the Admiral's staff, some of whom we had become very friendly with. And then the *Renown* slipped out of harbour, going east. We had spent nearly twelve months with the western Med fleet, carrying the Admiral's flag. Now we left both the Admiral and his flag behind.

The following morning we went on the upper deck to see where the sun was rising. Sure enough, it was over our stern. We were steaming west. The Tannoy speakers crackled and we crowded round to hear the news that we all hoped for.

'This is the commander speaking. Just to let you know that we are going to Rosyth in Scotland for our refit.'

The cheers that went up must have been heard back in Gibraltar. Not even the grey dismal day that greeted us as we sailed up the Forth could dampen our spirits as we looked joyfully forward to fourteen days' leave.

I finished relaying my experiences aboard the *Renown*. I was the toast of the town. You would have thought I'd steered the ship myself. 'An 'ero is what 'e is,' they said. 'A bloomin' 'ero.' I didn't feel like a hero. Funny thing was, all these people, who faced Hitler's onslaught on their homes and yet whose spirits couldn't be diminished, were all heroes to me. Somehow, my experiences seemed puny compared to theirs.

The party Dad threw for me seemed rather empty; many of our relatives were away serving and somehow I didn't feel right about celebrating my own homecoming without them. But one person I was very happy to see there was Benny, my older brother.

Benny was the brother I didn't know I had until I was at school. Two years older than me, he had been raised by my grandparents when my parents found it impossible to cope during those difficult days when I was just a baby.

My grandparents brought Benny up as thought he was their own son, and I came to know him as Uncle Ben. At school he took on the role of my protector — in those days I was often the target for gangs of bullies. He became my hero. He excelled in almost every sport and was signed on to play for Arsenal. But Benny, during my term of leave, was far from happy. His work exempted him from military service and I could see that he was being torn apart. Some people even accused him of cowardice. The final straw was when a young woman presented him with a white feather.

After that Benny disappeared and we heard nothing from him for a few days. Then we learned that he had joined the Navy. Because he had been signed on to play for Arsenal, he was offered the post of a physical training instructor, but he turned that down. He wanted to do his bit for the war effort and was happy to be sent to the Mediterranean to serve on board HMS *Naiad*, a light cruiser.

My leave was over far too quickly. I hated farewells and liked to get them over with quickly, so I said a speedy, 'Goodbye Dad.'

'Bye son,' he said. 'And remember — never volunteer for anything.'

His advice caused me a smile as I left to meet my shipmates at King's Cross station. Although I had enjoyed my leave, the train journey couldn't be over with too soon for me; I was looking forward to rejoining my ship. On route we each talked of the good time we'd had on leave, but that only served to make us feel homesick. My worries were not for myself but for the folks back home. We had the power to hit back at the enemy. They just had to sit it out. If they could take it, I decided, I certainly could. There was a war on, and a job to do, and I was keen to do it well.

We arrived back at the *Renown*, docked at Rosyth, passing the lads who were now off for their turn of leave. Much of my time after that was taken up with sentry duty, with the occasional run ashore to the nearest village. The ship was duly refitted and looked formidable with her new equipment. RDF masts bristled everywhere, and there were spanking new anti-aircraft guns and a few other additions.

Ready for sea again, we set off, as usual with no idea what our destination was. A heavy sadness lay upon the ship as we sailed down the Forth; each man wondered just how long it would be before he came home again.

The expected announcement came over the Tannoy. This time we were on our way to Iceland. It seemed that the *Tirpitz*, *Bismarck*'s sister ship, was about to put to sea again and our job was to protect the convoys to Russia from her.

Escort duty again! I hated the thought of it. I preferred to be in action rather than plod along with the slowest ship in the convoy.

Iceland loomed on the horizon and we slowly steamed into harbour at Reykjavik. The admiral's gangway was hoisted over the side. By now I had become regularly involved in this process and when the platform was in place I went over the side, kept from falling into the sea only by a line tied around me and held at the other end by a shipmate. Normally this task didn't bother me one jot, but on this occasion the rating on the other end was not known to be particularly quick-witted. However, I got on with the job, slipping metal pins, to help support the gangway, in the supporting stanchions. Finishing the job, I hung there for a moment, looking down in some fascination, watching the waters rushing against the ship's side. Before I had time to realize what was happening, the line somehow slipped and I went splashing into the freezing water.

Up above, the rating holding the other end had been too busy surveying the snow-capped mountains to be aware of the line slipping. The sudden jerk as I surfaced, gasping for air and yanking on the line, brought him to his senses. He frantically hauled me up. I had only been in the water for a few seconds, but it felt like ages.

I clambered on to the quarterdeck, shivering and spluttering and firing some choice words at the rating. No one seemed to have noticed my plunge into the icy depths; there were so many other harbouring duties being carried out. All I wanted to do was get below and change into dry clothing. The incident was quickly laughed off and I thought no more of it; but two days later I awoke in the morning to find everything revolving around my hammock. My head was throbbing unbearably and I could do nothing to shake off the dizziness. I decided I'd best report to sick bay. I climbed out of my hammock, and as my feet touched the floor, my legs buckled and I passed out.

I awoke in a cot in sick bay. Two days had passed. The doctor was standing over me. 'You've had a rather nasty touch of bronchial pneumonia,' he told me. I would have to stay in bed for another week at least.

During the next several days my Marine mess mates came to visit me and brought me magazines, but I felt too weak to cope with company or to read. My head hurt, my breathing was noisy, and all I wanted was rest. During this time, a peculiar thing happened. I had a strange notion concerning my brother, Benny. I had the feeling he was dead. I put the thought out of my mind.

One day the Medical Officer came to my bedside with some wonderful news: they were sending me back to England.

My spirits rose immediately at the prospect of some unplanned leave. The stretcher party carried me to the quarterdeck, where I was strapped into a cradle and hoisted over the side by crane on to a lighter. Then I was ferried to a cruiser where I was made comfortable in their tiny sick bay. That night we weighed anchor and headed for home, hoping that we would not meet with any unwanted action.

What we did run into was one of the worst storms in that area for many months. It was certainly the worst I'd ever encountered. The best that could be said about it was that it kept us safe from U-boat attacks. But being confined to bed, I felt especially vulnerable as the ship rose and dipped and rolled violently. I lay in my cot and prayed for the journey to end.

Finally, with the storm still raging, we arrived at Scapa Flow and after we dropped anchor I was transferred to a more comfortable hospital. After a few days the storm abated and we sailed for Aberdeen where I and other sick and wounded shipmates were ferried by ambulance to the hospital.

Day after day I was fed medicine and blasted with X-rays, and every other day the medic came to examine me, until at last he informed me that I was completely well and could be returned for duty. By then I was not sorry to be told I was well enough to go back into service; the doctors and nurses had all been wonderful but I was bored by inactivity. However, I had been granted fourteen days' sick leave.

I returned home, to the delight of my father and step-mother. During my term of leave, a telegram arrived from the Admiralty addressed to Dad. He tentatively opened it and read the terrible news: Benny had been killed. He had died during my time in Iceland; I had had a premonition of his death.

His light cruiser, HMS *Naiad*, had been dispatched to draw out the Italian Navy. But she was sunk, probably by submarine, and Benny had died with his shipmates.

This news filled me with anger. Now the war had taken my brother — my hero — and I blamed those who had sent him to the *Naiad*. I decided that I would fight no more. I was not going to return when my leave was over. I began hitting the bottle heavily, and nothing anyone could say could make me change my mind. And when my leave was over, I remained at home.

Dear old Dad, whose loss of Benny was no less than mine, sat me down and gave me some wise counsel.

'You must go back to your unit, son,' he said. 'If you don't, you'll be letting Benny down. You know he wanted to do his part. He'd want you to go back. If you do, you can get even. You can't run away. Go back to barracks, son.'

It was the thought that I could avenge Benny's death that brought me to my senses. I packed my kitbag and headed for Stonehouse Barracks where I'd been assigned, arriving two days late. Reporting to the company office, I was met by the most evil-looking sergeant major in the Marine corps, and the very sight of him told me I was in deep trouble. He told me how horrible I was and yelled and roared at me, finally confining me to barracks to await judgement from the Company Commander the next morning.

The next day I was marched before the Company Commander. 'Well, Marine Sparks, what have you to say for yourself?' he demanded.

I tried to explain why I had taken it upon myself to extend my leave and hoped he would have compassion enough to understand. But my words fell on deaf ears. 'You're confined to barracks for a week,' he said. I was promptly marched out of the office and duly confined to my barracks. I had to consider myself lucky to get off so lightly. But the next seven days dragged unbearably. I had nothing constructive to do; just the usual fatigues, spud-bashing, cookhouse duties, cleaning the officers' mess. I was bored to death. I began popping into the drafting office to see if they could find another ship for me.

Then, one morning, I was scanning the notice board when I came upon a call for volunteers for specially hazardous service. Something popped into my head: This, I thought, was a way of avenging Benny's death, although how I would achieve this I didn't know. I went straight to the Company office and, ignoring Dad's advice, 'Never volunteer for anything', I volunteered.

Days passed and I began to think that my request had been turned down. Then came the order to report for an interview. I turned up at the office and sat with the others waiting to be called in. Finally my turn came, and I entered through the door to be met by a major. He stood some six feet tall and, although he had lost much of his blond hair, he sported a huge flowing moustache. His blue eyes twinkled. I judged him to be an officer of the old school rather than a war-time officer. He was twenty-eight years old and spoke quietly, with an Oxford accent. There was something about this man that told me he was important and I couldn't help but feel in some awe of him.

'I am Major Hasler,' he announced in his soft voice, then asked a few concise questions. Besides the obvious one — 'Why do you want to volunteer?' — none of his other questions really made much sense to me. What I did understand was that if I was accepted, I would become a Commando.

'Can you swim?'

'Yes, sir.'

'Do you have any experience with small boats?'

'No, sir.'

'Are you married?'

'No, sir.'

He was, in fact, looking for unmarried men who possessed a fighting spirit, natural intelligence, resourcefulness and self-reliance. He knew that volunteers like me might end up behind enemy lines, where survival and success would depend equally on intense training and quick wits.

The interview over, Major Hasler thanked me and said I would be hearing from them shortly. So I left not knowing whether I was to be committed to fatigues for the rest of the war or not. The fact that

I had no experience with small boats was something I thought would go against me since he obviously wanted experienced sailors.

For the next few days I checked the notice board in case my name should appear on some list or other. Then it happened. There it was. My name was on a notice informing all those listed to pack kits and be ready to leave for Southsea the following morning. I felt ten feet tall. I was going to become a Commando. What I didn't know was that I was to be sent to almost certain death.

2

MY ORDERS WERE TO PROCEED by train to Portsmouth, and I duly arrived at Portsmouth on 23 July, 1942. There was quite a crowd milling around just outside the station, about forty Marines in all, and I joined the throng. I knew no more than any of the others as to what our purpose was in being there; this put us all on an equal footing and our expectations were high. The thought that this could be a mission from which we might never return did not enter our minds. It was a hot day, the smell of the sea was in the air and we were all caught up in the excitement of a new adventure.

A three-ton truck pulled up and we climbed aboard. It rumbled off and after a short while we came to a stop. 'Right, you lot,' ordered our waiting Colour Sergeant. 'Out!' We jumped down from the truck. 'Fall in on the beach. You're at the seaside.'

We promptly fell in on what turned out to be our very own private stretch of beach, out of bounds to all civilians and even to military personnel without specific permission. This, I thought, smelled of cloaks and daggers. But with the warm sun above and the cooling sea gently lapping at the sand, it was easy to feel as though we were here for some kind of activity holiday.

Colour Sergeant W. J. Edwards was a spotless, shiny Marine from the top of his head to the tips of his toes. He was no spring chicken; a still very active pensioner recalled from the reserves to act as our Sergeant Major. We soon learned that when you spoke to him you made sure you were standing to attention, and there was no calling him 'Colour', it had to be 'Colour Sergeant'. However, we also called him 'Bungy' Edwards.

Bungy had decided that he could show us youngsters a thing or two. But he was to prove very helpful to us all and did everything he could for us. In time we tried to get close to him, but he always kept us at arm's length.

We had been selected for special service, he told us, and were going to be training in small boats. I thought he meant rowing dinghies, which sounded like fun. This adventure was getting better by the minute. We all felt the same; we were young and we were going to have a good time. The fact that we'd be training for specially hazardous duties was forgotten.

We were just going to have a good time playing with these small boats! However, Combined Operations, headed by Lord Mountbatten, had not brought us here to enjoy ourselves, although we had no idea what military operation awaited us, nor yet that the author of that operation was Major Hasler himself.

To begin with, Bungy went on, we were to find our own lodgings among the civilian population, and for this, we would be paid an extra six shillings and eight pence per day. This all sounded very welcome, especially the part about extra pay, known as Commando subsistence.

I could have been forgiven for thinking that this bonus might turn out to be no bonus at all, for I recalled that during my first weeks as a Marine recruit, I had what I thought was extra money coming at me left, right and centre. The day I was sworn in at the recruitment office, I was given half a crown. Before embarking for Deal I received another half a crown. Five shillings bonus so far, with more to come.

Before our first pay day came around, we were informed by our drill instructor that we were to draw some extra money. We marched smartly to the pay office and, one by one, passed the window to collect our five shillings bonus. So far His Majesty's Government had given me ten shillings, and I still had my weekly pay of fourteen shillings to come.

With our new five shillings jingling in our pockets, we were marched round to the NAAFI and found waiting for each of us a yellow duster, a tin of metal polish, a block of green blanco and a tin of boot polish. Purchase of these items was not voluntary, and the lot cost us five shillings each.

Still, we had fourteen shillings pay to look forward to and when the day came we eagerly fell in to march round to the pay office. I waited patiently in line until I came to the window. I gave my number and held out my hand for the fourteen shillings. The pay clerk dropped the coins into my hand; four shillings.

'Four bob?' I said. 'What about the other ten shillings?'

'Did you not previously receive ten shillings?'

'Well, yes,' I said, counting up the two half crowns I'd been given, plus the five bob to pay for the duster and polishes.

'Then you've had your fourteen shillings — ten shillings plus four,'

'Yes, but...'

'Ten shillings was an advance of your pay, not a hand-out. Now move on.'

I felt conned. But they were the sort of setbacks recruits came across, and I had no need to concern myself over the Commando subsistence of six shillings. It was a genuine bonus, and life looked even brighter when Bungy Edwards announced that he had already found lodgings for us all.

'All right, you lot, back on the truck,' ordered Bungy. We climbed aboard once again and set off on a mystery trip round Southsea. Our first stop was in Worthing Road. Bungy read off a short list of names: 'Ellery, Fisher, Moffat, Ewart, Sparks...'

I jumped down with the other men called and we found ourselves on the pavement outside a house called White Heather. This was to be our home for the coming weeks, Bungy said. He led us indoors where we were met by our landlady, a rather jolly Welsh lady whom Bungy introduced as Mrs Powell. But what caught our attention was the sight of her very attractive sixteen-year-old daughter, Heather.

Mrs Powell's husband was in the Royal Marines, serving at this time in HMS *Aurora*, and Heather believed that she and her mother should accord us the same treatment they would give Heather's father. Therefore, when Bungy had first found the house and told Mrs Powell to take up the carpets so we couldn't ruin them, Heather convinced her to leave the carpets down.

Among our group, there was one who was particularly struck by the sight of pretty Heather and her caring manner — Robert Ewart. He was from Glasgow and naturally we called him Jock. He was quiet, tall and bony. Heather was to become equally struck by him within a very short space of time.

Being thrown together in this secretive situation and close proximity, we were, on the whole, to become good mates. Eric Fisher, from Birmingham, was a very likeable chap who was slightly older than the rest of us. He had a great deal in common with Yorkshireman David Moffat and they became particularly good friends. Both came from Irish families, Eric didn't smoke and didn't drink. David was surprisingly careful with his choice of words for a man in a Commando unit, and I rarely saw him drink alcohol. But he had a great sense of fun and occasionally earned himself a march on the double for his delight at sending up an NCO. We called David 'the Preacher', not

25

because he was religious but because when he sold you anything he gave you a sermon on it.

One of my best friends was Bill Ellery, perhaps because, like me, he was a Londoner from Soho. He was a marvellous swimmer, a very good medic and a fine footballer — I believe he'd had trials for Chelsea. In fact, he was a generally all-round good man that you could rely on to be right there with you when the need arose.

Collectively, we were No. 1 Section.

That evening all sections gathered on our private beach, separated from the rest of the world by barbed wire. It was an informal occasion, to allow us to get to know each other. We were something apart from all other servicemen. We were given the cover name of the Royal Marine Boom Patrol Detachment and the civilian population was led to believe our sole purpose was to patrol the six-mile boom which stretched from Lumps Fort to Seaview in the Isle of Wight.

Major Hasler gathered us around and addressed us without formality. 'Now, I know you all want to do your bit, but you are by no means in yet, not by a long shot. There are some eliminating exercises to go through yet, and I'm certain that our numbers will be very much depleted by the end of the day. Training will begin in earnest tomorrow. But for the rest of this evening, you can relax and get to know each other.'

Major Hasler, even Bungy Edwards, had given us all a vastly different kind of welcome to the one I received as a young recruit arriving at Deal to begin training. At the station, I was met by an old Marine who had been recalled to the colours for the duration of the war. He seemed friendly enough, but he must have seen me coming a mile off.

'You look like someone who wants to get on in the Marines,' he told me, making me feel immediately welcome. 'Now I'd say you'd be looking to make lance corporal as soon as you can, and I can help you, lad. You see, you want to impress the officers with nice, shiny brass buttons, and to achieve that you need a special gadget. And it just so happens I have some of these gadgets on me and I can let you have one for just six shillings. Now what do you say? Are you ready to part with such a paltry sum to become a lance corporal?'

Naturally I handed over the money and in return he gave me the 'gadget'. It was made out of tin and opened and closed like a pair of scissors. With this button-cleaning gadget, he assured me, I could not

26

fail to make lance corporal very soon. What he forgot to say was that, regardless of this gadget of his, he was still a private after twenty-two years in the Corps. He also forgot to tell me how the thing worked — and, of course, I soon found out that it didn't!

Together with the other recruits I was then taken to the barracks where we were to sleep on small iron beds with straw palliasses and straw pillows. Here the old soldier had another piece of good advice for me. 'Make sure you're up as soon as you hear reveille,' he said.

'What exactly is that?' I asked.

'It's when the drummer comes round in the morning at five o'clock.'

'Drummer?'

'Yes. But I'll bet you a shilling you won't hear the drummer.'

I thought about that. How could I fail to hear someone banging on a drum at five in the morning? 'All right,' I said, 'you're on.'

My uncomfortable bed gave me a restless night. At five thirty the next morning I was woken by a bugle. Everyone was crawling out of bed and getting dressed, so I did the same. I felt terrible. The old soldier approached me and asked if I'd heard the drummer.

'No, I must have slept through it,' I said. 'Can't see how I could have missed it.'

'That's a shilling you owe me,' he said, and I promptly paid him.

Another thing he had neglected to tell me; buglers were referred to as drummers.

He had one more trick to play on me. On the way to the wash-house he said, 'Use the hot water sparingly. The boilers have to supply the whole barracks and if the officers get no hot water, there will be hell to pay.'

'I'll just dash in and have a quick shower then,' I said. 'So long as the water's hot, it shouldn't be too bad.'

'That's a good lad.'

We reached the wash-house. The showers were running, so I thought I'd better be quick before the hot water got used up. After such a short night's sleep, a shower was just the thing to wake me up. I stripped off, dashed in and came to a dead halt, trying to gasp but finding my breath completely stifled. The water was like iced needles. The old soldier roared with laughter. At least it woke me up.

I slept like a log that first night at White Heather. I felt fit and ready the following morning to begin training. We fell in on our beach where Major Hasler, or 'Blondie' as he was known — though not necessarily to his face — introduced us to our small boats. 'This,' he announced, 'is a two-man collapsible canoe.'

Our hats nearly flew off. We knew we were going to be training in small boats of some kind, but we certainly didn't expect such flimsy craft. They were sixteen feet long, almost twelve inches deep and nearly thirty inches wide. When collapsed, they were only six inches deep. This proved to be Major Hasler's Mark I model.

'Right, men, into your swimming trunks,' ordered the No. 1 Section senior NCO, Sergeant Samual Wallace. A regular from Dublin who had seen almost twelve years of service, he possessed an engaging sense of humour and a strong Irish accent. He was full of so much cheerful determination that even when we felt exhausted he inspired us to keep going. Occasionally, though, he was too enthusiastic. I heard that when the Admiralty needed to discover how long a man could keep afloat in full gear, Wallace volunteered without a second thought. Dressed in full uniform and tin hat, he jumped into the sea and trod water for five minutes before sinking. He was a man we all had great respect and affection for.

We bundled into a bell tent erected on the beach and changed into our trunks. 'This is the life!' we told each other as we lined up on the beach, ready for the fun to begin.

'Right, men, let's see how you cope in the canoes.'

We had been put into pairs; I was partnered with Eric Fisher. The first group of men picked up their boats and waded into the shallows. The Major watched in obvious dismay as they displayed no sense of boatmanship whatsoever, trying to jump into their canoes and overturning them. The rest of us watching from the beach found it highly amusing, but the Major's face sank along with the boats.

I was relieved to see that I was not the only man with no experience with small boats; in fact, none of us had. Men with relevant boating skills had all been assigned elsewhere, not allowed to volunteer for this new unit. Blondie had to rely on his own ability to teach us all how to work these canoes. In fact he had to bear the burden of training everyone himself in boat work, including the officers assigned as instructors who were as ignorant as the rest of us. So included in our class was Lieutenant Jack Mackinnon who was in command of No. 1 Section. He was a Glaswegian, broad and athletic, fond of the open air and with a real love of life. He was a top officer, having served in the ranks before earning his commission. He was eager for action against the enemy and just as eager to learn how to cope with these canoes. It was reassuring to see that he was as raw as we were when it came to boats.

'Come on, Eric,' I said, 'This can't be too difficult.' We picked up our canoe and happily paddled into the sea. Trying to keep the canoe from floating away, we clambered into it, struggling to stay upright.

'Steady, steady!' I cried as I felt the canoe rolling. Suddenly it spilled us both into the sea. Fortunately I was a reasonable swimmer and I held on to the canoe for dear life. Like the others, I was desperately keen to make the grade.

Salvaging the boat was a two-man job — or should have been. Eric was having trouble salvaging himself. It turned out that he couldn't swim and only his lifejacket saved him from drowning. While I was concerned about the boat, all Eric thought about was Eric! Unfortunately Eric was a square peg in a round hole. He really didn't fit in at all, and if there was anything that could go wrong, Eric did it. Lieutenant Mackinnon later tried to teach Eric to swim, and while he barely managed to stay on the surface, he later became a frogman and gave good account of himself in a raid on Leros.

Many of the crews had been tipped out of their boats and had to wade ashore, dragging their half sunk canoes with them — provided they were able to retrieve them. The afternoon was spent salvaging the boats we managed to sink.

As time wore on, some of the officers were able to take over much of the training. Blondie relied heavily on Captain Jock Stewart, a London-bred Scot who had served with the Major in Norway. Even before the unit had been formally organized, Blondie had chosen Stewart as his second-in-command. We called him the 'old man'; he was almost thirty. I don't believe Blondie ever had any thought of sending Stewart on the actual mission, but as an instructor Stewart was to prove invaluable and took part wholeheartedly in every aspect of the rigorous training programme.

But until he was ready to take on the task of training, it was left to Major Hasler to teach us how to assemble the canoes until we could finally do it blindfolded, and how to paddle efficiently, which proved far more difficult than it looked. We also had to learn how to navigate at sea from a canoe, out of sight of land.

One of our earliest exercises was to find our way into Chichester harbour where, when getting out of our canoes, we ended up waist-deep in mud. There would be many times during the operation when we would encounter soft, deep mud banks which were impossible to walk on. Blondie taught us to manoeuvre over the mud by using the canoe like a sledge.

Fitness was paramount, so the Major decided we should run up and down the beach each day. None of us minded running, but on the first day we were a little shocked when he told us to remove our shoes and socks. It was a pebble beach, and those stones were hard and harsh against our bare feet.

We began the arduous and agonizing quarter of a mile run. It was absolutely crippling for us — all, that is, except Jock Ewart. He might have been skinny but he was tough as old boots, or at least his feet were. While the rest of us groaned and moaned as the pebbles pummelled our feet, he skimmed across them as though he had feet of leather. He was first home; in fact he beat us all every time. He possessed a keen determination to succeed and whatever he set out to do he invariably did with tremendous vigour. It was not surprising that during his time in the Boys' Brigade he won all manner of prizes. His eagerness to serve his country was such that he turned down a job in a munition factory to join the Marines, and when posted to the Orkney Islands he found life there too boring, so he volunteered for Major Hasler's unit.

The thing I enjoyed the most was unarmed combat. Perhaps there was a little bit of the wild boy in me, having come from the tough East End of London, but I'd always been active and I thoroughly enjoyed getting into a scrap with someone. Unfortunately some men got hurt quite badly, and those who ended up with broken arms or legs were promptly dispatched to hospital and then returned to their units; by the time such injuries were repaired, the other members of the group were too far advanced in their training. It was heartbreaking for some of those men, especially those who had excelled in so many skills, to be returned to their units because of a broken bone.

But I knew how to take care of myself. I'd had to learn quickly because back at Deal our physical instructor was the Corps heavyweight champion, who delighted in demonstrating his prowess. My turn came to assist him in his demonstration, but I turned up late that day because I had been to see the Depot dentist.

When I arrived up at the gym, the PI roared, 'Where have you been?'

'To the dentist,' I explained, hoping that this would excuse me.

'Right,' he said, 'get into your shorts and join me.'

I quickly changed and then he said, 'Right, you lot, I will now demonstrate the right cross. Like this.' He landed a punch on my face. 'Come on, Sparks, put your guard up.' I did. He landed another right. And another. And so it went on. I was determined that I would learn how to defend myself, and eventually I did. Now that I was training to be a Commando at Southsea, unarmed combat had become second nature to me. Nobody landed a right on me quite so much, and I could give as good as I got, if not better.

Practising bayonet drill often proved an amusing activity for us because of Sergeant Wallace's strong Irish accent. He would shout the order, 'Long point at the throat — thrust.' But this invariably came out as 'Long point at the t'roat, t'rust,' and we roared with laughter. Fortunately for us he had a sense of humour, and so long as we did the drill properly he didn't mind being the subject of our mirth. He was always the first person to laugh at himself whenever his canoe tipped him out into the sea.

We built our own assault courses under the guidance of our PTI, Sergeant King. Apart from this side of the training, King played no part in the eventual operation, although he was later awarded the Distinguished Service Medal in the raid on Leros. To build our assault course we used old tyres, ropes and anything else we could think of, but often with disastrous results. Our improvised equipment sometimes collapsed just as a man leapt on to it or through it or under it, and the injuries were sometimes severe enough to have the victim rushed to casualty.

Eventually the hospital complained that they were getting too many casualties from the RMBPD. To Blondie, this was all water off a duck's back. He didn't take any notice of anybody. He had mapped out a course of action and nobody was going to make him deviate from that.

We learned to live off the land, to discover what can keep a man going in times of urgency. This meant learning how to thieve! Especially from farms. On one occasion we came across a chicken farm and helped ourselves to a few of the plumpest birds. We made camp by a stream and merrily plucked the chickens, letting the feathers flutter into the stream and drift away. We lit a fire and roasted our mouth-watering booty. Unfortunately for us, it turned out that the feather-filled stream ran down past the farm where the chickens came from. When the farmer peered into the stream and saw the feathers floating by, he hurried back to his house and got his gun. Armed and angry, he went looking for the poachers.

We were munching happily on bits of wing, leg and breast when the farmer came upon us.

'You chicken thieves!' he cried, raising his gun at us. 'I ought to shoot you all. I'll blow you off the land."

'How do you know they're your chickens?' we asked him.

'Of course they're my chickens,' he ranted.

'Prove it.'

The poor man had no proof as we'd just eaten the evidence. Nevertheless, we felt it prudent to get off his land as soon as lunch was over.

We also learned that things that look repulsive can actually be quite edible — hedgehogs, rats, worms (worm omelette is particularly nutritious if you can steal the eggs) — so we would never starve to death.

Back at White Heather, we were well looked after, especially by Heather who despite her tender years took a motherly interest in us all. She darned our socks and mended our clothes, provided we were prepared to help out in the kitchen. She also ensured that we all wrote to our families regularly.

Between her and Jock Ewart, or Bobby as she called him, there was a deep affection growing. But just how much she loved Jock, nobody would know until after the operation was over.

The officers initially lived in Eastney Barracks, but had by now rented a small furnished house. Blondie moved in with them although he had been staying with his mother at Catherington. Some of the officers joined the rest of us in the evenings for a drink and a sing-song at Eastney Tavern. Officers fraternizing with the men was generally frowned upon, but between us it helped to build a real comradeship, and we had no less respect for men like Stewart or Mackinnon for it.

Blondie rarely joined in these jubilations but preferred to take out his own sailing boat, sometimes with a female friend. Private sailing was severely limited, but he overcame this obstacle by wearing his uniform. If a lady was with him she had to wear a Wren's hat. The patrol boats came to know this trick and when sighting him the men would say, 'There's Major Hasler with a popsy. Shall we look the other way?' Invariably, they did.

It had been summer, beautifully warm and sunny, when we began training, but inevitably summer changed into autumn, and then came winter. It made no difference to our training programme. We swam each day, even when the sea was freezing. We ran along the beach even when the pebbles were covered in snow. And we went out in our canoes even when the waves were high.

The winter sea could be deceiving. We once set out on a flat calm sea. Just off Southsea, the seas blew up very rough, very suddenly. Within minutes we were in the midst of a full six or seven gale, battling with waves that threatened to engulf us, struggling to remain upright. But the heaving sea was too much for us and every boat capsized. However, the Major did not allow us to take the easy way out and remain inland. Regardless of conditions at sea, he took us out in our canoes until eventually we learned to ride the waves, turning our bows into the waves just as they were about to break. By mid winter we had became expert canoeists, and we were not deterred by the most ferocious weather conditions.

During the first couple of months, we had used the Cockle Mark I. This canoe had a habit of developing leaks, so the Mark II was introduced. It was very much like the original Cockle but more robust. Even in the calmest sea, propelling these canoes throughout the night, as we often did, was exhausting. Most of the strain was on the shoulders and arms, and apart from regular arm-strengthening exercises, we had to rest every hour for five minutes to prevent muscles from being strained beyond their limits.

Despite the arduous training, we were by and large a happy unit and there was a real spirit of comradeship among us. We took great pride in ourselves. We wore no distinguishing marks, not even the green berets of the Commandos. When we marched into Eastney Barracks for lessons at the Signals School, we marched in a special rapid manner devised by Sergeant Wallace which we called the Southsea Stroll. Because we were obscured by secrecy we were looked upon with disdain by the other officers, although some tried desperately to discover what Major Hasler and his secret unit were up to. To most of them we were just 'Major Hasler's party' — end of story. They treated us with contempt, and when they had the chance to get one of us on our own, they used rough, though not violent, tactics to try and learn what we were up to. When word got back to Hasler that one of us had been bullied like this, he jumped up from his desk, got on his motorbike and drove into barracks to sort them out — he didn't care who they were; brigadiers, generals, whatever. In his eyes his boys could do no wrong.

Inside the barracks we were forbidden to use the NAAFI because we were billeted in civilian lodgings. However, this was not enough to deter Bill Ellery; he knew how to con his way through life. One day he disappeared into the NAAFI, leaving us outside and wondering how he expected to purchase anything that was out of bounds to us. A short while later he came back out carrying half a dozen bars of chocolate.

'I've got a rule in life,' he said, handing out the bars. 'Everything you *can't* have, I *will* have.'

He was fearless in a typical Cockney sort of way. Walking through the streets one evening, we stopped short as the sirens sounded. The Luftwaffe were on their way. We began running — except for Bill. All about us people were heading for their shelters as the German bombers roared overhead. Not Bill.

'I'm not running from the bloody Jerries,' he announced, walking off down the middle of the street, as calm as you like. The Luftwaffe roared overhead. Bombs were falling. But Bill stood his ground, raised his fist to the skies and yelled, 'G'on out of it! Clear off! Bloody Jerries!'

Reckless? Maybe. Courageous? Definitely. If I made it all the way through to the operation, I hoped Bill would be there behind me.

We were exceptionally proud of ourselves and the unit, although our pride sometimes got the better of us. We thought we could lick anybody in a fight, and we were prepared to prove it. On occasions we found ourselves being ridiculed by the sailors. Marines and sailors would always fight — if there was no one else about. It was a pastime for us. We loved a good fight; it took the monotony out of a life of constant training. Jolly Jack Tar only had to say a wrong word or move a glass of beer that belonged to one of our men, or any little thing, and over went the apple cart.

Nine times out of ten we were outnumbered. We'd find ourselves in a pub full of sailors, and there would probably only be half a dozen of us, but that didn't prevent us from picking a fight with them. I often came out of a foray with a black eye or busted nose. But it was all in good fun. Fighting was a part of life in those days. Nobody tried to kill anybody. If you punched someone and he fell on the floor, you helped him up and hit him again. There was no kicking a man when he was down. The fight would continue until either we were exhausted or the Military Police turned up. They'd break up the fight but nobody ever got carted off to jail because the MPs understood this friendly rivalry.

Gradually, through injuries, through men being assessed unsuitable, and through men who just gave up, the process of elimination resulted in our numbers being pruned to just those who would from now on train specifically for the mission ahead. Bill Ellery, Eric Fisher, Sergeant Wallace, Jock Ewart, Lieutenant Mackinnon, David Moffat and myself made the grade.

Completing the twelve men were Corporal A. F. Laver, Corporal G. J. Sheard, Bill Mills, James Conway — and of course Blondie. Laver was a regular from Barnet, a man of quiet demeanour, fair-haired, round-faced, often keeping himself apart from the evening drink-and-singalongs. He had been present at the sinking of the *Bismarck*. Sheard was short but tough and often witty, a Devonshire man. Surprisingly, he was married and his wife was expecting their first baby. Blondie must have thought him invaluable to have included him despite his own rule that only unmarried men could volunteer. Marine Bill Mills, from Kettering, was a high-spirited lad, stocky, fit, excellent at football and swimming. He could always do a good turn if needed and was better educated than most of us. He had a girl he loved. I enjoyed his wit and love of life, and he and Bill Ellery became my two closest friends in the unit. Marine James Conway, from Stockport in Cheshire, loved swimming, cycling and his horse. Before the war he had been a milkman with a horse and cart. He would talk to his horse as though it were his best friend and he missed it. Yet here, among men training for a mission that might well end in death, he was happy, and his fondness for the rest of us resulted in all of us being fond of him.

Blondie himself would, naturally, lead us. We were the twelve men who, the Major concluded, would best execute the coming mission. We were highly trained — with further training to come

— and we were, above all else, a single unit, dedicated to each other and to the Major.

Having survived the basics, we now started training in earnest for the job. We knew our task was to attack shipping. What we didn't know was where this shipping would be.

I had returned from leave a little late, as was my policy, but this time I was going to go before Blondie.

'When you come up before Major Hasler,' roared Sergeant Wallace, 'you can expect the punishment to be severe.'

I turned up at the Major's office, wondering what punishment he would have in store for me.

'What's the excuse?' he demanded.

'Well, sir,' I said, 'as I was going to Waterloo station by tube, the air-raid siren went and the underground trains all stopped, so I was held up, and by the time I got to the station the last train was just disappearing round the bend, sir.'

'So?'

'So there was nothing else to do but go back home and catch another train in the morning. Which is what I did, sir.'

'It didn't enter your mind then that if you'd stayed on the station you could have caught the milk train and got here on time?'

'No, not really, sir.'

'You knew the milk train ran?'

'Yes, sir.'

'Let's be fair. In other words you thought "Bugger them down there, I'm going to have another few hours".'

I stood there silent. He said, 'I'm talking to you.'

'Yes, sir.'

'Yes, sir, what?'

'Yes, sir, I did think "Bugger them", sir.'

'Do you know what I'm thinking?'

'No, sir.'

'Bugger you and all. Three days' pay docked.'

This punishment did not seem at all severe to me, for a few years before I had found myself facing the possibility of the ultimate punishment — a firing squad.

We were sent on armed night-time beach patrols. At such times we lived on the coast in tents. During one evening patrol I was on

36

duty, waiting to be relieved, when we had an alarm; a motorboat had been spotted in the vicinity and it was thought that enemy agents were about to land. Everyone stood to for about an hour, then marched back to their tents. All but me. Somebody had forgotten that it was time to relieve me. Since it was forbidden to leave your post, I had to remain there, hoping the Corporal would soon discover me.

It grew dark. There came another alarm and another stand to. Again no enemy landed and we stood down. I managed to attract the attention of the NCO and told him I was long overdue for relief.

'Very well,' he said. 'Remain at your post until you are relieved.'

I remained at my post throughout the night, feeling increasingly sleepy. My eyes were heavy, but I struggled to stay awake. Morning came. I heard the crunching of feet and saw, coming towards me along the shore, a patrol. Dutifully, I challenged them and asked for the password. They replied correctly and continued on their way.

The next thing I knew I was being nudged in the ribs. I had dropped off to sleep. In a panic, I reached for my rifle, only to discover that it was my own rifle that I was being nudged with.

Standing above me, holding my rifle, was a grim-faced officer. 'Get to your feet man,' he roared. 'You're a disgrace, falling asleep on duty. This is a most serious offence. You could be shot.' I was immediately put under close arrest, and after twelve terrifying hours the Adjutant arrived. 'You realize that you can be shot for sleeping in the face of the enemy,' he said. 'What do you have to say for yourself?'

I explained about the long hours I had stood guard. He listened to my story and in the end completely exonerated me. But I had never been so afraid as I was that day, waiting to hear my fate.

After that, the prospect of having my wages docked held no terror for me. It was just inconvenient. However, Blondie never did dock my wages. He could talk to you in your language and threaten you and really put the frighteners on you, but he rarely carried out his threats. Although when the occasion really called for it he could be a strict disciplinarian, he actually hated to punish anyone unless it was absolutely necessary. And as long as we pulled our weight and put every effort into our training, he would forgo punishment at every opportunity.

Blondie, as it turned out, was the man I got to know better than anyone else in the company. He eventually decided that Eric Fisher and I couldn't get on, so he made me his own Number 2.

Eric, in my opinion, should never have been in the unit. He was a wonderful man but prone to getting things wrong. For me, probably the last straw was during an exercise in which we had to deal with two-man torpedoes. This required us to drop a 5lb depth charge from our canoe and paddle away like blazes. The drill was for the Number 2, in this case Eric, to use pliers to crimp the end of the charge to set the fuse, drop the pliers into the canoe and throw the charge overboard.

We moved into position. 'Target in sight,' I said.

Eric crimped the fuse, dropped the charge into the canoe and tossed the pliers overboard!

After a great deal of panic and shouting, he grabbed the charge and threw it out before it exploded. So from then on I was with Blondie on all the exercises. This produced a whole new set of problems for me. The others could get themselves 'lost', in the loosest sense of the word, and end the exercise early. I had to see it all the way through every time. But then, Blondie usually knew what they were up to.

When we were training for an attack on shipping, he kept us all close together in our canoes, because he knew they would skive if they could. They said to me, 'You're sitting behind him. Tell him we've had enough.'

I tried my best. 'Getting a bit late in the day, sir,' I told Blondie.

'Oh, plenty of time yet; twenty-four hours in a day. Right, let's get on with it.'

The boys later complained at me for not getting the exercise called off.

In November we embarked on a large-scale exercise; we didn't know at the time that this was to be a dummy run for what was in store. The exercise had been code-named 'Blanket', and the plan was for us to start out from Margate, penetrate the defences of the River Thames and endeavour to get into London unseen as far as Deptford. London's defenders had been alerted that we were coming, firstly to ensure we didn't get shot at, and secondly to make us more careful since they would be keeping a sharp eye out for us. Any boat spotted would be challenged, and in that event we were to give the password 'Blanket'. The distance we were to cover would be around seventy miles.

We loaded our new improved Mark II Cockle canoes and stores onto our truck and set out for Margate. There we were temporarily billeted in a public house, of all places. Fortunately, we were only there for a few hours, most of them spent in the bar with the locals. Seeing that we were all blacked up with camouflage cream, the locals were convinced that we were going on a real raid, and they insisted on buying us rounds of drinks. We could have all got very drunk, but we refrained. They slapped us on the back and said, 'Give them one for Margate.'

Major Hasler briefed us and then spent the rest of the evening with Mackinnon working on the tide tables for each boat. At midnight we left the pub and made our way to the jetty where our canoes had been unloaded. Light-headed with beer, we launched our canoes and climbed in, ready for five full days of paddling. The sea was kind with just a slight swell. It was pitch black with not a star in the sky, so our compasses were our only means of direction finding.

We cast off, heading for the Isle of Sheppey where we were to navigate the narrow waters of the Swale, which lies between the isle and the mainland, and emerge into the Medway and back into the open sea. But as dawn broke and the Major and I found ourselves in the mouth of the estuary, just off the Isle of Sheppey, we realized we had lost the main party. Whether this was by design on the Major's part, or an accident, I never knew, but he was very keen that the men learn to stand on their own feet and make their own decisions. We were not to see them again for the rest of the exercise.

We quickly found a place to lie up for the day, and when darkness came we launched our canoe, ready for the next stage of the journey. We encountered patrol boats, some moored amidstream, others under weigh and most likely looking out for us. But we proved too canny for them, and on the fifth day we finished our exercise without having been spotted or challenged.

Back in Southsea, the Major learned how the rest of the party had fared. They only managed to get as far as Blackwall, short of the objective, too exhausted to go on and having been challenged at least twice each. Some had proved disastrous at navigation.

Mackinnon had run aground on mud-flats when leaving the Swale and by the time he had managed to release his canoe by twisting and turning it, he had lost his sense of direction, so he ended up going back exactly the way he had come.

Corporal Sheard had lost his way altogether and instead of going up the Thames Estuary he went down it. He had assumed he was following our canoe at a distance, and had been surprised to see our canoe suddenly fly up and away into the sky. Then he realized he had been following a seagull!

At the meeting to discuss the exercise, Major Hasler was in a foul mood, and spared no breath in telling us exactly what he thought of us. Despite all the training we had let him down, he said. We obviously were not ready for operations.

This was deeply upsetting as we had begun to think ourselves ready for anything. Equally dispirited, Blondie returned to Combined Operations Headquarters in Whitehall to report the failure of Blanket to Lord Mountbatten.

Mountbatten, though, proved not so downhearted. 'In that case,' he told Blondie, 'you must have learned a great deal from your mistakes, and you'll be able to avoid making them again during the operation.'

Our training continued at Southsea, now doing underwater exercises, for as well as everything else, we were trained to be frogmen. But before long, following the Margate-to-London fiasco, Major Hasler decided to move us all up to Scotland, in the Clyde. Perhaps he had decided that Southsea was a little too soft for us. Certainly the prospect of training in the wilds of the Clyde gave a sense of greater urgency to the whole training operation. It was 19 November when we arrived; we had no way of knowing that there were only ten days ahead of us to complete our training.

Our loch was very secluded. It was a submarine base, complete with a submarine depot ship where we kept all our ammunition and limpet mines. From this ship the subs would replenish their stocks of food and ammunition, including torpedoes. The HMS *Forth*, where Blondie had expected to put us all up, turned out to be full, and so we were lodged aboard the *Al Rawdah*, an Indian merchant ship moored nearby. It was rather luxurious compared to our usual sleeping quarters.

Canoeing and swimming in the lochs of Scotland was a different proposition to Southsea. I had never felt so cold. It always seemed to be on the point of freezing up there. And yet, because we had become used to swimming every day, we were able to withstand the cold of the lochs. We had certainly been toughened up, and the cold wasn't enough to prevent us from walking around with open-neck shirts whenever possible. It was important that we reach our peak of fitness. Our main protection from the wet and cold was our 'cockle suit'. Camouflaged and waterproof, each suit had an elastic skirting that stretched over the top of the canoe's cockpit to make an efficient cover. Under the trousers we wore long woollen pants. On our feet we had gym shoes over which we wore thigh-length waders. The jacket covered several layers: a woollen vest, a shirt, a sweater and a scarf, and also an inflatable lifejacket under the main jacket. Two pairs of gloves and a Balaclava helmet completed our outfit.

We embarked on a forced march over the island of Bute, tramping over the mountains, trying to find our way as far as possible without using the compass. The result was that we got ourselves totally lost. But I was surprised to discover how subconsciously we could remember a mound or a rock, and after a number of attempts we learned how to find our way back.

During this and subsequent expeditions, we were introduced to our main armament, the silent Sten gun, an amazing piece of work which was like the ordinary Sten except that it had a silencer tube on the end of the muzzle which resulted in just a very faint click when the trigger was pulled.

I was a fine shot by now. But when I took my first turn on the rifle ranges at Deal, I had proved to be abysmal with a gun. When it was my turn on the butts and I fired my first ever round of .303 ammunition, I couldn't understand how I managed to miss the target. I had taken such care over lining up the sights before I squeezed the trigger. Besides, the recoil was horrendous. I felt like I had been kicked. But, grimly determined, I tried again. Then I looked up and saw a flag being waved across the target.

The instructor loomed over me. 'See that flag, Sparks?' he asked. 'That flag is being waved because you missed the target altogether.'

I protested that the sights on my rifle must be faulty.

'Really. Give your rifle to me.'

I handed him the weapon and he fired off five rounds in quick succession. The bull's-eye was practically blown to bits as the bullets tore into it.

'It would appear,' said the instructor, 'that the fault is in you.'

After that, it took me only a few days to master the rifle and I qualified as a marksman, as all Marines were required to do.

Training in Scotland was all hard work. There were no runs ashore for a drink in the local, for there was no local, no place to go. So we made our own amusement, trudging over the mountains, strangely enough, as though we hadn't had enough during the day. We hoped to celebrate the birthday of Bill Mills — his twenty-first — on 11 December, not knowing that we might get sent out on operations before that.

Submarines now became part of our training. We sailed out into the North Sea and practised embarking and disembarking from the subs. I soon grew to hate being inside those cigar-shaped coffins and was only too happy when we would at last surface to begin our exercises with the canoes. We'd all grown very fond of our little craft; we had learned to sleep in them, eat in them and literally live in them for days on end.

One day, with our canoes fully laden, we began to disembark from the submarine but discovered we could not launch the canoes properly. Whenever we put a canoe over the side a wave would hit it, so that the canoe sometimes ended up resting on the side of the submarine where the next canoe would hit it. Major Hasler decided that we needed some sort of crane, and he came up with the idea of fixing a steel bar underneath the submarine gun which would then hoist the canoe off the casing of the sub, fully laden with stores and its crew, swing it over the side and lower it into the sea, two or three feet away from the side of the submarine.

Our naval engineers did a wonderful job on Blondie's idea and we put to sea to try out the equipment. As Blondie and I were hoisted up by the gun turret and put out over the side, I must admit to finding it all rather scary. We were held dangling above the sea, hoping that Jolly Jack was keeping his wits about him, swinging in mid air until we were clear of the submarine. But it all worked very well.

We practised this exercise time and time again until we were perfect, for there could be no second chance for any of us when the time came for the real thing.

Our main toy was the limpet mine. We had to attend a series of lectures to learn what it was all about and how to assemble it. It consisted of a block of high explosive, encased in a metal box measuring approximately fifteen inches by three, to which were attached several magnets. When placed on the hull of a ship, the magnets would cling to the metal and, at a given time, the mine would explode and so punch a hole some four feet wide in the side of the vessel.

The fuse was chemical, encased in a tiny glass ampoule that would be broken by a thumbscrew. The acid would gradually seep its way into the compartment containing the explosive, and so detonate the mine.

At the other end of the mine was a synthetic fuse, a very delicate piece of work that was designed to activate the mine in the case of another mine exploding prematurely, thus ensuring that all the mines exploded together. None of us liked this type of fuse because if they were knocked while in the canoe they would result in us having a bird's-eye view of the explosions. To activate the charge, the igniter on the end of the time fuse was squeezed with a pair of pliers.

During our course in demolition, one sergeant put some explosive in a little tin and said, 'No way can this ignite by a flame. It's got to have a primer in. And I'll prove it.'

He took out his cigarette lighter, struck it and put it to the explosive. We all winced but he was confident. Suddenly there was a bang and a cloud of smoke. As the smoke cleared we discovered all his eyelashes had gone. It proved that you should always treat explosives with respect — but we nevertheless came to treat them with some contempt, paddling along in our canoes with these mines lying between our legs.

When the lectures were over we had to continue training with the mines by using them on ships. There was a Dutch ship, an old coaster, which used to cruise round the lochs, and we had to chase him in our canoes to simulate tidal racing and then attack him with limpet mines. We had special magnetic holders to attach ourselves to the ship while we placed the mines.

The buzz now was that we were going after the *Tirpitz* up in Norway, although of course the limpet mines would have been useless against that particular ship. They would have virtually bounced off her hull.

One morning we boarded the depot ship to find ourselves being instructed by a colonel in how to camouflage our canoes. He drew chalk lines all over one of the cockles and advised us as to the colours that should be painted. We then got to work drawing the required chalk lines and painting them battleship grey. Then the names of the canoes were painted in small letters on the bows: *Catfish, Crayfish, Conger, Cuttlefish, Cachalot* and *Coalfish*.

The rumours began to spread again. It was obvious something big was about to happen. By now we were convinced that we were going after the *Tirpitz*. When the Major heard that we had figured out we were going to Norway, he warned us that rumours have a very nasty habit of being true.

'There, you see,' we reasoned, 'it's true, we *are* going to Norway.'

We spent some time going over our gear, ensuring that all our arms were in perfect working order. Then we sewed our shoulder flashes on to our cockle suits. These consisted of the Combined Operations badge with its triple union of anchor, rifle and wings, and the shoulder badge reading *ROYAL MARINES*. Officers and NCOs carried rank badges. All this was to show, should any of us be captured, that we were soldiers to be treated as prisoners of war under the Geneva Convention.

On 1 December we arose early, as usual, and were ferried over to the depot ship. There our canoes, looking very smart in their new camouflage, awaited us. All the equipment was there, including automatic pistols, fighting knives, whistles that sounded like a seagull's cry and, assigned to the canoes of Hasler and Mackinnon, two silent Sten guns. Alongside the ship was the *Tuna*, our T-class submarine. As far as we knew this was to be a day like all the others; just another exercise.

All our stores were loaded on to the *Tuna* and we fell in on the upper casing. Then, to our surprise, the submarine fleet commander came on board and addressed us.

'The day that you have all been training for has come. I don't know where you're bound or what the job is to be. What I can say is that people of the highest authority are awaiting the results. Good luck to you all.' He then returned to the depot ship.

We stood still and silent in single file as the submarine pulled away from the depot ship and her long black hull slid out towards the North Sea. The still was sounded; we were being saluted. We knew then that it had to be something big.

3

WE WERE ORDERED BELOW DECKS and told to gather in the forward torpedo room. Major Hasler awaited us. On a blackboard he'd chalked a map of France. The surprise on our faces to see a map of France instead of Norway was not lost on him. 'So sorry to disappoint you,' he grinned. 'We're not going to Norway after all. We're going to France.'

He knew that the rumours had been flying around concerning our eventual destination; I'm convinced he encouraged them to some extent. But now it was time for the truth. The grin faded.

'This is the real thing,' he said soberly, and he went on to explain what our mission was.

The Germans, he told us, had a fleet of fast, armed ships — blockade runners — operating from the safe harbour of Bordeaux, and running to Japan. These ships were too fast for our submarines to catch. To send in planes to bomb them was out of the question because it would have to be high-level bombing and thus liable to be inaccurate; a lot of French people would get killed by our bombs. So Combined Operations had decided to send someone in to blow up these ships. That someone was us.

The Major paused, allowing us to gather our thoughts. I was very pleased that we were not, after all, going to Norway; I'd figured that this was going to be a trip with a one-way ticket, and if we were going to have to scuttle our canoes and make our way back by other means, Norway seemed such a long way from home. But France somehow felt closer, almost on our doorstep. I think all the men felt the same.

The Major went on. The submarine would take five days to reach the point where we would be put over the side, somewhere in the Bay of Biscay, some ten miles to the south of a headland called Pointe de Grave where a lighthouse marked the entrance to an estuary. Then we were on our own. Passing between the headland and the small island of Courduan, we would paddle up the estuary of the Gironde some sixty miles to the port of Bordeaux. And there, it was hoped, we would find the blockade runners.

The mission was code-named 'Operation Frankton'. It would take us five days to paddle up the estuary, travelling by night only, lying up during the day, camouflaged on the river banks. Naturally we'd have to avoid all contact with the locals; one small word in the wrong ears could bring the enemy looking for us.

We would travel in convoy for the first night and then split up into two parties of three canoes each. When we reached the target area, the first section, led by the Major, would attack the south side of the harbour whilst the other section, under the command of Lieutenant Mackinnon, attacked the north side.

Aerial photographs had been supplied, the Major continued, and he issued us each with a complete set. The photographs showed, in sections, the whole of the river, so that we could choose the best lying-up places. We were also issued with a list of French phrases which the Major though might help us get out of trouble if the need arose; he was the only one of us who spoke French.

'This is just 'Blanket' all over again,' he said to reassure us. 'It's going to be tough, but we can do it. Are there any questions?' No one spoke.

'Well, these are the plans for getting in, so I'm surprised that not one of you asked about getting out. So here is the bad side of the operation. Because it will take us five days to get to the target area, when the job is complete it will naturally take five days to get out again. By which time, of course, the balloon will have gone up and the Germans will be searching high and low for us. We can't ask the submarine to wait all that time for us or she may be discovered herself. So, when the job is complete, we will paddle back downriver for about five miles, and there we will scuttle our canoes and make our way across land for the escape.'

I knew it; we did have only a one-way ticket.

Plans had been laid for our assistance, the Major continued. After the raid, we would have to split up and each crew would have to make their own way across land. We would all get a bag of escape gear, and we'd have to travel on foot to a little town called Ruffec; this would take about a week. Once there, we had to find the Café de Paris, where we would wait until one of the French underground agents made an approach. The Resistance had been told that we were coming, and when we were sure these people were the genuine thing, we should leave the rest of the escape plans to them.

'One more thing,' he added. 'Anyone who gets into trouble will be on his own. One man's peril must not jeopardize the operation, and there will be no exceptions to this rule. I realize that this is a bit more than I originally asked of you, so if any man thinks that he is not quite up to it, let him speak up now. I assure that no one will think any the less of you for it.'

We looked from one to the other and grinned. The Major didn't show it but he must have been delighted. Sergeant Wallace piped up. 'If I get captured,' he said, 'I'm going to declare myself neutral, because I'm Irish!'

What we didn't know then was that Lord Mountbatten, knowing that the survival rate was expected to be nil, had not wanted Blondie to lead the operation himself. But the Major had persuaded him that he must be the one to lead us. And he was right, because we would have followed Major Hasler anywhere.

Since he was a boy, H. G. Hasler had possessed a passion for boats. At the age of twelve he built his first two-seater canoe in partnership with a friend at school. Off the Hampshire coast he learned the basics of navigation and at fourteen he designed and built a sailing boat on his own. Several years later, as a second lieutenant in the Royal Marines, he cruised single-handed in a sailing dinghy from Plymouth to Portsmouth over five and a half days, and later made the return voyage in six days. As well as being a keen seaman, he was inventive, creative and an individualist.

In 1941 he wrote a paper on methods of attacking enemy ships by canoe and underwater swimmers. It was rejected by Combined Operations, a unit conceived by Churchill in which the Army, Navy and Air Force worked together to develop ways and means of launching raids on enemy installations of all kinds. In January 1942 he found himself assigned to Combined Operations Development Centre at Southsea. His new boss was Mountbatten. His assignment was the study and development of all methods of attacking enemy ships in harbour. This included investigating the Italian explosive motorboat and the two-man torpedo-shaped submarine called a chariot. But what intrigued him most was the idea of the canoe as an assault craft. Despite the rejection of his ideas the previous year, he had since discovered that certain special forces in Britain and in the Middle East had already used canoes in operations against enemy coasts, and with some success.

He began studying all known types of canoes available in the UK, trying to find a craft that could be launched from a submarine; but none of them displayed the sort of characteristics he sought. He decided that a new canoe had to be designed. He did, however, adopt the First Special Service Brigade's own technique of blowing up enemy ships with magnetic limpet mines attached to the ship's hull by a six-foot rod. By this method, they had sunk a large enemy tanker in Boulogne harbour.

But the type of canoe they used, much like the Cockle Mark I, failed to satisfy Hasler. (Later he consulted a Mr. Fred Goatley, who had won a War Office competition for his design of a river-crossing assault boat, and together they created the Cockle Mark II.)

He proposed to Combined Ops that he be allowed to start a new unit in which he would himself train men to use the canoe as a weapon. This being accepted, he embarked on a course of training for himself, navigating dark waters in a canoe, patrolling the coast throughout the night and getting ashore undetected; the first two attempts resulted in his capture by patrol boats, but his third attempt was successful.

On 9 May, 1942, Lord Selborne, Minister for Economic Warfare, wrote to Prime Minister Churchill informing him that enemy ships were running our blockade and that, since Japan's entry into the war, traffic between Germany and Japan had increased. Lord Selborne wrote further on the subject in a letter to Mr Attlee, the Deputy Prime Minister. The problem was referred a few days later to Combined Operations. Meanwhile Lord Selborne's ministry discovered that enemy blockade runners were harboured at Bordeaux. The activities of the runners in previous months had resulted in the transportation from the Far East to Germany of thousands of tons of crude rubber, tin, tungsten and other materials important to the German war effort. German cargoes were likewise being shipped to Japan.

The solution to this problem, Mountbatten reasoned, was possibly Major Hasler's special canoe force, and he wrote to the Chiefs of Staff Committee asking for their approval of Operation Frankton — which in time became more commonly known as Operation Cockleshell.

The eventual outcome was that, with the other members of this operation, I was now on board the submarine *Tuna*, heading for the south-west coast of France.

There was even time to rehearse the hoisting out of the canoes from the *Tuna*, but this turned out to be our last chance to get some fresh air. As the sub nosed her way towards the Bay of Biscay, the sea swelled and rolled in a Force 4. Because submarines have no keel, the *Tuna*'s rounded bottom caused her to roll heavily from side to side; I was sure she would roll right over, but that's about the only trick she didn't perform in the heaving seas. I expected my old malady to overcome me as she pitched and dived, but thankfully I was one of the few not stricken this time. Most of my Marine mates were dreadfully sea-sick and even some of the submarine crew were ill.

Our remaining days on the submarine were to be filled with intense briefing, but the stormy sea conditions were too rough to allow any kind of training. Our sleeping quarters, among the stores in the forward torpedo room, were not exactly comfortable for those who were ill, and even when the sickness wore off, some of the men were badly hit by bouts of claustrophobia. Unused to life on board a submarine, sea-sickness was aggravated further by limited sanctuary facilities and the foul air that gave us headaches and made us drowsy.

On the third day we reached enemy waters, and with the threat of attack from the air, we submerged. It was a relief to get beneath the waves, not least because there the boat was calm. We spent some time practising a few French phrases which the Major thought would be useful. This kept us all amused as we tried to get our tongues round the unfamiliar sounds; but little, if any, of it would help us if we found ourselves in real trouble. Meanwhile, of course, over and over again, we discussed, examined and dissected the whole operation until it was firmly etched in our brains.

During the day we stayed submerged, occasionally coming to periscope depth so that Captain Raikes could take a look around. We encountered a number of enemy patrols who were on the surface while we just cruised along safely beneath them. Then came the time when the Captain ordered action stations. We had encountered a German U-boat.

A dangerous game ensued in which we stalked each other. The submarine crew kept us informed by giving a running commentary on what was happening. Inside a submarine you can see nothing of what's happening outside the hull, but you can hear a bit. At one stage we were puzzled by what sounded like a motorbike going past.

'That was a torpedo just missing us,' explained one of the crew.

That brought us all out in a cold sweat, but the crew just took in their stride.

It became almost unbearable, sitting there in the mess, with nothing to occupy us while every member of the submarine crew had a job to do. We were used to being able to hit back, but all we could do was sit around listening for another torpedo and try not to think of the consequences.

Then we fired off a torpedo. 'One hundred and eighty feet,' said Raikes. 'Hundred and eighty feet, sir.'

In the mess there was a depth gauge which we were glued to, and we watched it fall and hoped that we would eventually come back up again. Then came the sound of another torpedo. It roared safely past.

'Hundred feet,' said the Captain.

We watched the gauge rise and gave thanks. It was the worst part of the journey and we were all thankful to be alive when finally we lost contact with the U-boat.

At last the day arrived, 6 December, when we were to be put over the side to commence our operation. Shortly after midday the French coast was sighted. Preparations for disembarking began. Waves of excitement and anticipation ran through the boat. We were itching to get going. The submarine surfaced, rolling heavily. We had run into yet another of the Bay of Biscay's furious gales. It needed all the Captain's skills to keep the boat upright.

But it was impossible for us to launch our canoes. The excitement waned and our spirits dropped. There was one consolation in the storm; there would be no enemy surface ships about.

We prayed for the seas to subside, but there seemed little hope of that. We had to remain on the surface that night so the submarine's batteries could be recharged. As dawn approached there was still no sign of a calm. We had no choice but to go to diving stations and once more we submerged beneath the waves.

The day was interminable as we waited for night to fall. At 7.30pm we prepared to surface, hoping and praying that this time the sea would be kind. With a crash, the submarine broke through the surface and came to settle on an even keel. Several anxious minutes passed while we waited for the roll that would prove our prayers in vain. It never came. The storm had abated. The sea was as calm as a mill pond.

'Major Hasler on the bridge,' came the Captain's voice. Hasler disappeared. Several anxious minutes passed. We were ready to go – we just awaited the order. The Major returned. 'Right,' he said, 'prepare to disembark. It's on.'

We were almost bubbling over but managed to contain ourselves, to concentrate on the task of disembarking. The forward torpedo hatch was opened.

'Up canoes,' ordered Captain Raikes. Each canoe crew was responsible for hoisting their own craft through the hatch and onto the upper casing, assisted by members of the submarine crew. The gunners stood closed up at their gun with its bayonet-like steel rod protruding from beneath the barrel, ready to act as our crane. Our canoe, *Catfish*, was first up on the casing.

The Major and I took our places in the canoe and commenced to stow our limpets in between our legs. Then came our special compact ration which was to last us a week, together with two cans of drinking water. There was no turning back now. Our boat was tackled to the gun turret. Soon we were aloft and being slowly swung out over the water. Gently lowered, with just a slight splash, we were on the surface of the sea, about two feet away from the submarine. We pushed ourselves out from the sling which was hoisted back up, ready for the next canoe. The second, third, fourth and fifth canoes joined us. Laver and Mills were in *Crayfish*. Sheard and Moffat were in *Conger*. They, with us, were in 'A' Division, under Blondie's command. Mackinnon, with Conway as his No.2 in *Cuttlefish*, led 'B' Division, including Wallace and Ewart in *Coalfish*.

Then came the terrible news, hailed to us from the submarine. *Cachalot*, Bill Ellery's and Eric Fisher's boat, had knocked against the hatch clamp, tearing an eighteen-inch long gash in its canvas side just above the water line.

Blondie was grim-faced as he called up to Bill and Eric. 'I'm afraid you can't go. You must abort your mission and return home with the submarine.'

'Let us try sir,' pleaded Bill.

'You'll fill up with water and sink.'

'We can bail out fast enough, sir,' Bill argued. 'And in the morning we'll be able to mend it.' He gave every argument he could think of, but the Major knew it was hopeless. Before he had finished his futile argument, Bill was in tears as Blondie made it clear that there was no time for further discussion. Like all of us, Bill and Eric were keyed up, and this had come to them like a slap in the face.

There was nothing we could do but leave them behind as we began our mission. Bill and Eric stood on the upper casing. 'Good luck,' they called through their tears.

Our five canoes formed up, with Major Hasler and myself in the lead, and we began paddling towards the mouth of the Gironde. We heard a slight roar and, turning, saw the black hulk of the submarine sliding away. We were alone.

On the shoreline, lights blinked from the farm houses. It made the coast look somehow more friendly, I thought, with the coast so well defined by these lights, somebody obviously didn't realize there was a war on. Or maybe the Germans were so cocksure of themselves that they were convinced that their defences could not be penetrated.

The Biscay swell lifted us slightly as we made our way in the direction of the estuary. I could see the lighthouse on Pointe de Grave, and hoped it would not be an enemy to us.

It was bitterly cold. The heavy-laden canoes rode low and the spray of small waves broke over our cockpits, freezing into a frosted coating. Even so, I was damp with sweat.

We paddled in silence. All I heard was the breaking of the bow wave and the gentle splashing of paddles. Communication was by hand signals, and the canoes had to remain close enough to see any signals being passed. Occasionally we had to close up, or raft up, and hold on to each other's craft to enable the Major to whisper orders.

After about an hour or so we were struck by the vague sound of roaring ahead. We stopped paddling. The Major signalled for the other canoes to raft up. We were bewildered by the strange rushing noise. But the Major told us that this was a tidal race, the point where several currents of water meet.

'It's going to get pretty rough,' he whispered, 'but don't worry. Just treat it like rough weather and we'll soon be through it.'

We secured our cockpit covers tightly and Blondie and I headed into the tidal race. Suddenly we found ourselves tossed about like a cork, as though we were in rapids. We fought desperately to control the canoe with our paddles, finding this far worse than any rough weather we had ever encountered. Four-foot-high waves, monsters for any canoe, crashed down on us from all directions. I felt sure we would be swamped as we bucked and turned, fighting with all the skills we'd acquired just to keep the canoe upright. Then, just as suddenly as we had entered the race, we were in steady waters again. We were panting as we turned about, waiting for the others to come through.

Laver and Mills arrived and rafted up to us. Then came Sheard and Moffat, followed by Mackinnon and Conway. But there was no sign of Wallace and Ewart in *Coalfish*.

'We'll go back to look for them,' Blondie told me, and we turned back into the surging waters in search of the missing canoe. I blew the whistle which hung about my neck, making the cry of a seagull. If they had capsized, the canoe would at least have stayed afloat for a while, and we all wore lifejackets. But there was no sign of them, no sign of the canoe, no answering cry to my call. They had vanished into the night.

There was the leaden feeling of loss – loss of our friends and of a third of our force. We returned to the others, signalling the hopelessness of further searching, and continued on our course. We paddled fast and after a short while there came the unmistakable roar of another tidal race. This time we approached it with far more apprehension and caution than before, but almost without warning we were in the boiling waters. If anything, they were more turbulent than before. The waves reached five feet, breaking over us, threatening to engulf us. Our tiny craft pitched and bucked, tossed about like a matchstick. I felt sure that this time we would capsize. Then we were in calmer waters again.

We waited for the others to catch up with us. A second canoe arrived, followed by a third. Anxious moments passed as we waited for the fourth. But it never came. This time it was *Conger*, with Sheard and Moffat, which failed to appear. The Major and I headed back into the torrent, searching for the lost crew. Again I blew on my whistle, and the other two crews, hearing the seagull call, decided to pitch in as well, joining us in our search despite the ferocious waves.

We found *Conger* capsized; clinging to it were Sheard and Moffat. We rafted up.

'Hold on to our stern,' Blondie told Sheard. 'Moffat, take hold of

Cuttlefish.' The men in the water grabbed at our canoes, blue lips trembling.

I tried to turn the canoe over, as Blondie told me, but it was full of water and impossible to refloat. 'Very well,' he said grimly, 'you'll have to scuttle her.'

We managed to retrieve some of the mines and shared them out between the two other crews. Then I took my clasp-knife and began to slash open the sides of canoe. Within seconds *Conger* had sunk.

It was around two in the morning and we were falling behind schedule. The orders had been plain; no man's jeopardy should put the mission in peril. The Major was having to make swift decisions, and I could see that he was tormented. He could not just leave the two men there to fend for themselves in the freezing water. They would die for sure. The beach, we knew, would be infested with the enemy and to try to reach it in order to save Sheard and Moffat would result in almost certain capture or death.

He decided to tow the two men in as close to the beach as possible. 'Hang on,' he told them.

The weight of the men in tow made the going slow, but at last we were approaching the mouth of the estuary. The revolving beams from the lighthouse swept over us, illuminating us with each revolution. At any moment we might be sighted and fired upon. But no shots came. Now the tide gave us a helping hand, carrying us round the Pointe de Grave and into the Gironde. Only twenty minutes had passed since we had found Sheard and Moffat – it seemed like hours – and both men were weak with exhaustion and shivering with cold. Time was against us. The tide would soon be turning and we would be swept back into the bay. The Major had to make a terrible decision. He ordered us to raft up.

'I'm sorry, but this is as close to the beach as we dare go,' he told Sheard and Moffat. 'From here you will have to swim the rest of the way.'

He knew that they would be lucky just to make it to the beach in that cold sea; they were already frozen through. But he tried to sound optimistic. 'I wish we could take you further, but if we're all caught the operation will be at an end, and none of us want that. Get yourselves ashore, make your escape overland as best you can.'

'It's all right, sir,' said Sheard. 'We understand.'

The two lads reached up to shake hands with us and wish us luck.

God knows it was they who needed it. Laver took out a flask of rum and handed it to Sheard. Before leaving the submarine, unknown to Blondie, the crew had given some of us a flask of Pusser's Rum. But he made no comment. He just looked down at Sheard and Moffat and said, 'God bless you both.'

The two lads let go of the canoes that had kept them afloat for the past half hour. We paddled away. It was too painful to look back at them. Blondie's heart must have been heavy. He knew he was leaving them to their fate. I could hear him sobbing.

All around us in the mouth of the estuary there was ·intense activity. It seemed as though the Germans had chosen this night for a defensive exercise. We didn't know it then, but their radar had picked up our submarine as we were disembarking and they were even now sweeping the waters with searchlights.

Intelligence had warned us to expect a patrol boat at the mouth of the estuary, and sure enough, looming out of the darkness, there it was. But we were shocked to see that behind it was another. And a third. It was now too late to circle around the danger area. There was nothing for it but to press on, hoping to dodge the three boats. Again we rafted up. The Major gave his orders. We had to go through one at a time. Single paddle, lowest position. Above all we had to be quiet. The Major and I went first, crouching low, our faces almost touching the cockpit cover. The only sound we made was the dripping of water from our paddles which we separated into single paddles as we slid silently past the first boat. So far, so good. We came to the second patrol boat and began passing it. Suddenly, it began sending a signal to shore with its lamp. We kept paddling, hardly daring to breathe. Then to our horror we saw that there was a jetty ahead which we were going to have to pass, and on it stood a sentry.

We paddled on, drawing close to the jetty and hoping against hope that the signalling had nothing to do with us. Drops of sweat washed the camouflage cream down my face and into my mouth. It tasted bitter. My throat was pepper-dry from fear – fear, apart from anything else, of failing the mission. It made me more cautious, more careful in everything I did. That's what helped to keep me alive. In fact, I had never felt so alive. All my senses were keener, sharper, more acute that at any other time in my life.

We passed the jetty and then the third boat. I still expected to hear gun shots. My back felt exposed. But the shots never came. We pulled up to wait for the next canoe.

Crayfish with Laver and Mills appeared like a ghost alongside us. Laver gave the thumbs up sign.

We were making quick mental calculations as to where Mackinnon and Conway in *Cuttlefish* should be, and estimated they should be just about drawing level with the second patrol boat. At that moment the second vessel began signalling to shore again. I could feel my heart pounding in my ears as we sat in stupefied silence, willing the third canoe to appear.

From the jetty came a shout. A single rifle shot rang out. Then there was silence. We waited, knowing that by now the third canoe should have appeared. But it hadn't. We gave the seagull call. There was no response.

During that first night we had lost two-thirds of our strike force. It began to look as though the operation was doomed to failure.

The author shortly after he was awarded the DSM in 1943.

No. 1 Section; the section that never came back.

Colonel Hasler, Mary Lindell, Countess de Milleville, and the author
at the presentation of a scroll to the Countess by the Royal Marines.

The author and Colonel Hasler revisit the Dubois family who
sheltered them during their escape.

4

SERGEANT WALLACE AND JOCK EWART had completely lost their way in the first tidal race. They had not capsized as we supposed, but had been tossed about so much in the turbulence that their sense of direction became confused. Wallace was all for going on, despite the odds, even though, as he had demonstrated during Blanket when he followed a seagull, he was not perhaps as skilled a navigator as some of the others.

Young Jock Ewart seemed not to believe he was not coming back, at least up until the time the operation began. He had written to his parents. 'I've a feeling I'll be like a bad penny, so please don't upset yourselves about my safety.'

Back in Southsea Heather had received a number of letters from him which he'd written while training in Scotland, and all he spoke about was his longing for the day when he came back to her. She had bought him a cigarette case for his birthday and wanted to send it on to him. An NCO had told her to wait until he came home. But Heather was not convinced that her Bob was coming home. When he and the rest of us had said our farewells to her and Mrs. Powell to leave for Scotland, Heather had cried and told her mother, 'I just know they will never come back.'

The last thing on the minds of Wallace and Jock was getting home. All they could think of was continuing with the operation, and they paddled on towards the estuary.

It was around 4.00am when the sea rose up against them again, and once more they found themselves fighting swirling currents, buffeted on all sides by cascading waves. They made a valiant effort just to remain upright, but the surf was too much for the canoe. It rolled over and they tumbled into the sea. Wallace could make out the lighthouse on Pointe de Grave not too far off, and they swam in its direction.

The swim was exhausting but with ebbing strength they made it ashore, dragging themselves onto the beach. Nearby was a flak battery of the Luftwaffe. The Germans saw the two Marines and quickly descended on them.

In Gascony, Captain Max Gebauer, the senior naval officer of Inshore Squadron, was informed of the capture. The previous evening he had been dining with Admiral Buchmann, Commander-in-Chief of Western France, when news came through that a British submarine had been picked up on radar. The capture of the Marines now prompted Gebauer to order an immediate search for any other British parties. Down by the estuary, searchers retrieved the capsized canoe as well as limpet mines and maps. Meanwhile, the prisoners were handed over to Gebauer. In keeping with Hitler's Commando Order, Buchmann told Gebauer that Wallace and Ewart were to be shot. News of the prisoners reached the Paris headquarters of von Rundstedt, from where orders were dispatched to the German Army to take immediate action in the defence of the U-boat base at Bordeaux.

The prisoners were brought before Buchmann who noted their uniforms, each with the Royal Marines shoulder title. It was clear that these men were not spies and should be treated according to the Geneva Convention. But he was bent on carrying out Hitler's command that all British commandos be executed. However, intelligence officers wanted to interrogate the prisoners, so Buchmann agreed to allow the officers time to do their work.

Wallace and Ewart were taken to the old French fort at Royan, on the north bank of the estuary, and there they were interrogated. Neither man gave anything away. In fact, on the night of 8 December a call was put through to Colonel von Tippelskirch, at Hitler's battle headquarters in Poland, by Rear-Admiral Wilhelm Meisel who felt that the interrogation had so far failed; he wanted to bring in a special interrogator.

'The Führer's orders are quite clear,' von Tippelskirch told Meisel. 'The men must be shot at once.' Meisel argued that the men should first be interrogated.

The following morning, von Tippelskirch's superior, General Warlimont, called Meisel's headquarters and said, 'On the express orders of the Führer, the captured men are to be shot after first being questioned – with no methods barred.'

It was a couple of hours since we had left Sheard and Moffat to fend for themselves in that freezing water. The tide was beginning to turn, making paddling ever more difficult as we continued towards our target, keeping close to the west bank. I had never felt so mentally and physically exhausted. It was early morning and it was obvious we would make no further headway, so we began to look for a place to lie up for the day. Spotting a suitable site, we headed towards the bank but found our way obstructed by a row of half submerged stakes over which the swell broke. In danger of being thrown against them, we had to summon our last reserves of strength to keep going upriver.

Eventually we spied what appeared in the dark to be a small island, and we cautiously edged towards it. Hitting the beach, the Major quickly jumped out of the canoe to reconnoitre the land beyond while we remained in the boats. Before long he reappeared out of the darkness, signalling that it was all clear and for us to beach the two canoes.

We hauled the boats clear of the water and began camouflaging them. Our limbs were stiff and cramped. We were soaked through with perspiration but nevertheless chilled to the bone. Blondie could see that we were tired, but he ensured the job was done properly. We laid the canoes next to each other among the bushes, and covered them with camouflage netting and covered that with branches and leaves. Then we decided it was time for the Englishman's beverage, a cup of tea. We were well provided for this. We had a special burner, a sort of paraffin block with a tin tripod on which we could place our billy cans, which was powerful enough to boil the water for a decent cuppa.

To eat, we had special compact rations like compressed fruits, compressed cheese, compressed meat, hard biscuits, sugar, powdered milk and tea. But at that moment, all we wanted was a hot cup of tea.

We finished our tea and climbed under the net to take our places in the canoes, having removed the cargo bags so that we could lie down, two in each boat, stretched from bow to stern. Within minutes we were asleep. All except for Blondie. Good man that he was, he remained awake to take the first watch.

Dawn broke and we awoke to stand to, ready for any patrols that might come our way. It was bitter cold, so I pulled out my flask of Pusser's Rum and took a neat, warming swig. As I did so, out of the corner of my eye I saw Blondie glaring at me. Now I'm sure to get a rucking, I thought. But he just held out his hand, saying 'After you.' I gave him the flask. He took a mouthful and handed it back. He never said another word about it.

Just then, the sound of voices and pans clattering reached our ears, and looking around we saw a band of women and children, some with carts, heading towards us. At the same time, several fishing boats were emerging from a nearby small creek into the river. To our horror, a few of the boats turned and headed straight for where we were beached up.

The women and children came to within some fifteen feet, then stopped. We lay under our net, watching anxiously as the men from the boats came ashore and approached their womenfolk. This was not an island after all but a finger of land stretching out into the river at a place called Pointe aux Oiseaux. The creek the boats had just left would soon dry up as the tide went out; the fishermen had simply moved their boats into the safety of the river and were now about to have breakfast prepared by the women.

They chatted away quite happily. We silently prayed not to be discovered. Then their chattering ceased. All became quiet, and we realized that they had become aware of our presence.

'I had better go out and speak to them,' said the Major. 'I'll try and convince them that we're friends. All the same keep me covered.'

He rose from our hiding place, unbuckled his pistol and went over to them, addressing them in French. They looked surprised, suspicious, even frightened. Afterwards the Major said he had simply told them we were British and asked them, as good Frenchmen, not to say anything to anybody. But they still looked frightened. The Frenchmen briefly talked among themselves. We could not understand a word that was being said, but we could detect a little of what was taking place by the expressions on their faces and their general manner. It was evident that they did not all agree on what course of action to take. There was something about the Major that failed to convince them all that we really were English, although what it was that made them suspicious we would not discover for some time yet. Presently one of the fishermen told him they would say nothing; they had not seen us.

The Major returned to us. 'I think we'll be all right,' he said. We would just have to wait and see. We could hardly take them hostage and hold them all day; someone was bound to become anxious about them and come looking for them.

Finally, the fisherfolk finished their breakfast. The boats put out to sea and the women and children headed for home. We were alone again and wondering what the outcome might be. Our fear was that, even if the adults said nothing, one of the children might let loose a careless word. It seemed to us unlikely that of all these people not one would say something. The prospects if the Germans caught us were unthinkable.

The day seemed unbearably long. We ate some breakfast and managed to sleep on and off, taking it in turns to keep guard. The Major, as usual, took the first watch. I was due to relieve him. He told me he'd wake me in an hour for my turn, but it was four hours later when he shook me out of my sleep.

Bill Mills, my good friend, kept me company much of the time, but we said little about the operation itself. Our small talk was usually about our adventures ashore in Portsmouth and the fights we had won and lost. As we laughed over these escapades, the Major looked at me and said, 'If we're in trouble, we can always trust you to laugh over it.' For me, humour was a way of coping with the terrible uncertainty.

We had no way of knowing that at about this time Wallace and Ewart had been brought before Admiral Buchmann and would very soon be undergoing interrogation.

Dusk began to fall. It was the time, we knew, when the enemy would strike, if they were coming. We prepared to lift the camouflage and launch the canoes. The Major raised his night glasses for one last look round.

'Damn!' he cursed. 'Stand by, lads. They're coming.'

We peered towards the mainland shore line. Sure enough, there was a grey line of some fifty figures that appeared to be heading our way. We were hopelessly outnumbered.

Someone has given us away, I thought. We cocked our Sten guns, felt for our fighting knives and kept our heads low. They would not have an easy job getting us; we were going to put up a fight that would take a good many of them before they got us. This, I thought, was our last night on Earth.

We waited. Time seemed to come to a standstill. The figures seemed no nearer than before. Darkness covered the land. Why don't they rush us?

The Major lifted his night glasses, took another look, and then to our amazement he began to chuckle.

He's flipped his lid, I thought. This time I couldn't see anything to laugh about.

'It's all right,' he said cheerfully. 'Stand down. Those enemy soldiers are nothing but a row of anti-invasion stakes.'

'But, sir,' Bill Mills protested, 'they were *moving*.'

'Just a hallucination,' the Major said. 'It's not uncommon for men under strain to hallucinate in this way.'

The tide was at its lowest ebb and to launch our fully laden canoes we had to haul them for nearly a quarter of a mile across the muddy banks. By the time we reached the water's edge we were soaked through with perspiration and thankful to be waterborne once more. We paddled out to the middle of the river. It was pitch black; the moon was not expected for about two hours yet. This was an important factor in our plans and we had to make our way accordingly.

As we headed for the middle of the river a merchant ship passed by, obviously headed for Bordeaux. We tucked ourselves behind the ship and followed in its wake for a while until it drew away from us.

The tide would turn within the hour; then we could expect some help from the inrushing currents. We paddled at a fast pace, dipping the paddles into the water in an almost robotic fashion. Our actions were automatic, but our senses were keenly alert, especially our ears which we kept pricked for any sound of a patrol boat that could come at us from any direction.

It was freezing cold. Water found its way through our gloves, numbing our fingers. The sheer exertion of paddling nonstop, coupled with the little sleep we had managed to snatch, began to catch up with us. When the Major became aware that our canoe was no longer keeping a straight line, he realized that I was flagging and paddling much slower than he. He passed me a Benzedrine tablet. I swallowed it and before long I felt as though I could match any pace the Major set us. As Laver and Mills showed signs of exhaustion too, Blondie also revived them with Benzedrine.

Apart from the occasional rest, we kept up the pace for six hours, covering twenty-five miles. By the time dawn was about to break, we had picked up the east bank just north of Porte de Calogne. It was 9 December. We were more than ready for a day's rest as the morning light grew. The bank was strewn with hedges, perfect for our purposes, and we were able to pull right up against the bank, into a ditch hidden by bushes. The Major stepped ashore and disappeared for a few minutes to do his usual reconnoitre. He returned and said, 'Okay, haul out the boats and get them into the ditch, It'll give us good cover.'

We accomplished this quickly and lit our paraffin block burner to brew up some tea. Just as we were about to settle down, a little dog appeared from nowhere, jumping around us and yapping loudly.

'Bugger off!' I said. It ignored me. It didn't understand plain English.

Nothing we could do would shoo it away and its constant barking inevitably brought its master to investigate. He came strolling along, whistling, unaware of the danger he was in. We were ready to do whatever was necessary had he proved in any way to be hostile. He virtually walked on top of us. As four blank faces glared up at him, his whistling suddenly ceased.

The Major stood up and said his piece in French: 'We are British Commandos, here to do a job. As a good Frenchman, I ask you to say nothing about us to anyone.'

Again I was trying to read the Frenchman's expression; the Major was always careful to keep his own expression neutral and his face gave nothing away. The Frenchman became extremely excited, which didn't tell me much, but I figured he had to be friendly because otherwise Blondie would have disposed of him there and then.

The Frenchman began laughing. Blondie grinned, which was the most he ever did, and turned to us and said, 'He wants us to go and have a drink with him.'

'What are we waiting for?' I asked.

'Sorry, Bill, but not this time.'

'But this man could turn out to be a good ally if we stop and have a drink.'

Blondie turned back to the Frenchman and said, 'Thank you, but not today.' The Frenchman looked gravely disappointed. Blondie told him, 'After the war we will come back and have that drink.'

'When is the war going to finish?' he asked. It was a common question, as I discovered in the coming weeks. It was as though they figured that Churchill had personally sent us with the message: 'Tell the French people we will be over by such and such a date.' Blondie hated to disappoint these people when they asked, and so he always said, 'Very soon.'

The Frenchman was very enthusiastic and proceeded to shake us each by the hand. 'Bonne chance!' he cried. 'I hate the Nazis. Your secret is safe with me.' Then he left with his dog.

Well, I thought, he seemed friendly enough, but he might have been saving his own skin by pretending to be on our side. He might still betray us.

The day wore endlessly on and our confidence in the Frenchman grew. At the very least we were thankful to have remained undiscovered by the time darkness once again hid us from enemy eyes. We prepared to launch our canoes. But just then came the unmistakable sound of whistling.

We immediately took up positions, ready with our knives and guns if necessary. Out of the darkness stepped the Frenchman again. We breathed great sighs of relief. He approached the Major and said he had come back to see if there was anything we wanted. Blondie thanked him but assured him that we had all we needed.

Once more he wished us good luck, then he turned about and walked back into the night.

'Let's get out of here,' said Blondie.

We launched our canoes and set off once more. We had not gone far when suddenly, from ahead, we heard the throbbing of a patrol boat — and it was heading towards us. We quickly turned into the tall, thick reeds that lined the water's edge. Just in time. The boat slid by, its wake causing us to bob among the reeds. The throb of the engine disappeared and when the river became calm again we pulled out.

The night was full of activity. Patrol boats seemed to be out in force. We wondered if they might be looking for us. We didn't know it then, but they were indeed sweeping the river for possible saboteurs following the capture of Wallace and Ewart. Each time we encountered a patrol boat, we had to take to hiding in the reeds.

It was no later than 9.00pm and we had made little headway. The tide was ebbing and paddling against it became increasingly difficult and exhausting. There was nothing for it but to find a suitable hide. We pulled into a small unnamed island, which we christened Desert Island, close to the vineyards of St Julien and with an abundance of tall reeds. Here we waited and caught a little sleep, waiting for the tide to turn. It was around 3.00am when we were able to take to the river again.

As dawn caught us out, we were approaching the Ile de Cazeau, which was large for a river island. It was inhabited and stretched for about a quarter of a mile in length. It had no high reeds to give us cover, but was mainly flat and grassy. We pulled in to the bank and Blondie stepped ashore for his reconnaissance. It was 10 December.

A few minutes passed. Suddenly Blondie came racing back, hurriedly pushing our canoe back out again and jumping in. We had landed on an island used for anti-aircraft guns, he explained. The other canoe followed our example as we paddled quickly away.

It was now getting light and to continue any further would be suicide. We had reached the furthest tip of the island. Blondie decided we had no choice; we would have to land on the island and take our chances.

The bank was steep, muddy and slippery. We clambered ashore, hauling our boats up, our feet slipping and our clothes getting sodden and caked with mud. With no reeds to offer cover, we hauled our canoes away from the bank, carrying them to the middle of a field. There we covered them and ourselves with our camouflage nets.

And there we were stuck with no prospect of moving about at all. We couldn't even brew up some tea but had to remain sitting in our canoes, nodding into occasional sleep. That meant everything, including eating, even going to the toilet, had to be confined to the canoe. To urinate, we used a tin can which we then tipped over the side.

A little way ahead of us was a wood, its trees hiding one of the gun sites from the air. We were so close that we could hear the German gunners talking; therefore, we had to keep silent ourselves, for they would certainly have heard us.

Despite this, our spirits were high. We had, after all, been trained to spend days and nights in this sort of situation; it was nothing we had not expected. We were well concealed, although we could see out through the net quite clearly.

A short while later we heard the hollow clanking of a bell and the lowing of cattle. A herd had come into the field. And they were curious, gathering around us, looking through the nets with mournful eyes and sniffing at us. We made futile attempts to shoo them away. But they just stayed where they were, chewing the cud and poking their runny noses against the net.

The Major, sitting in front of me in the canoe, suddenly froze. I looked over his shoulder to see what had alarmed him so much, and what I saw made my heart skip a few beats. Standing at the edge of the wood were two German soldiers, looking in our direction. They were obviously curious about the gathering of cows around one specific area of the field. If they decided to come and investigate, the field would, without fail, run with blood.

Each of us trained our silent Sten guns on the Germans. God, don't let them come over, I prayed. If they did, we were prepared to open fire, even though we knew that it would bring their comrades down on top of us. That would probably be the end of the mission, and of us. But we would go down killing Germans.

I felt blood rising in my ears and sweat trickling down my face. We sat and watched and waited, but the soldiers made no move towards us. They must have seen us, I thought. Finally, deciding either that there was nothing of concern, or that they had no intention of putting their lives on the line, they disappeared into the woods.

But the day was not over, and we had to sit it out, unable to move or eat anything hot. We longed for night to fall.

We were not the only British Commandos encamped on the Ile de Cazeau that day. On the east side of the island, just a few miles from our own hiding place, were Lieutenant Mackinnon and James Conway. Blondie had always kept hope that these two were somewhere behind us and would eventually catch up. We had no idea how close to us they were. My own thoughts were that, after they failed to join us after passing the three patrol boats, they might have returned to try and rescue Sheard and Moffat. But in fact they had simply lost contact with us, although just how and why nobody knows.

They had not given up their mission after losing us, but had gone on alone, intent on catching up. They had never been far behind. On 10 December they reached the Ile de Cazeau and hid up for the day, as much at risk of discovery by the German gun crews as we were.

At 9.00pm they set off on the last lap of the journey, for the next day, the 11th, was when we planned to raid the shipping in Bordeaux. It looked very much as though Mackinnon and Conway would, after all, catch up and join us for the big event.

They had not been paddling for long, keeping close to the bank of the island, when suddenly the canoe shuddered to a halt. They had struck something submerged. There was a huge gash along the side of the canoe; water was pouring in and they began to sink. Mackinnon easily slipped out and swam away. Conway tried to follow but the stores and mines around his legs obstructed his feet. He kicked and struggled until he was free, then swam away just as the canoe with all its cargo sank to the bottom of the river.

They were still close to the island and had no choice but to swim for its bank. Despite their courageous efforts, the mission was over for them, and their only thought now was to escape.

Far up the French coast, at Brest, a body was washing ashore. It was David Moffat. There was no sign of Sheard.

That same day, there was an air raid over Plymouth; that's where Sheard's pregnant wife waited in the hope that he would return to see their first child. She was killed in the air raid.

Admiral Buchmann read the message that had come down from General Warlimont. Buchmann wanted only to dispose of Wallace and Ewart. But his orders read:

> With no methods barred, also using the subterfuge of
> sparing their lives and the assurance of good treatment, try
> to obtain before execution the following information . . .

Wallace and Ewart had spent the previous two nights in the Port of Royan, unaware of the messages concerning their fate passing between Royan, Paris and Poland.

At 4.00am on 10 December, guards entered their room and ordered them out. They were put in a truck, driven to Bordeaux, and there handed over to the Security Police which were to the original occupied half of France what the Gestapo was to the half which had only recently become occupied.

At their hands Wallace and Ewart were interrogated. By the end of it, all that the Germans had extracted from Wallace was that he had led a party of two canoes, one of which was damaged on the submarine. Neither he nor Ewart said anything that betrayed the surviving canoes which the prisoners hoped were now approaching Bordeaux armed with limpet mines.

The Germans issued an announcement that on 8 December 'a small British sabotage squad was engaged at the mouth of the Gironde River and finished off in combat'.

Darkness came at last on the Ile de Cazeau. The air was biting cold, frosting up our damp clothes. We removed our nets and, with all the stealth we could muster, hauled the canoes back across the field and down to the river. We lowered them down the steep, muddy banks and climbed in. We had already spent some twelve hours sitting in the boats; even so, it was good to be back on the river and pulling away from that island. Our nerves were frayed from waiting under cover all day with the threat of discovery hanging over us. Paddling somehow eased the tension, and we moved eagerly and urgently.

Leaving the Gironde behind us, we entered the Garonne on which lay Bordeaux. A steady drizzle, coupled with the slight wind that had blown up, deadened the sound of our paddles. For the first two miles we were able to keep to the centre of the river, but when we encountered heavy patrol boat traffic we moved in close to the bank, occasionally running for cover.

We were not far now from Bordeaux. We had almost arrived. The deed would soon be done. Then, if we were still alive, we could begin the journey back home. Now, France seemed no closer to home than Norway was. But I couldn't let myself think beyond the operation itself. That was all that mattered.

During the dark hours of the morning of 11 December, we found some tall reeds, six or seven feet in height, and decided that these would give us perfect cover for the next day. We were at Bassens South; not far ahead lay Bordeaux harbour. Our cover was so good that at dawn, after managing to sleep a while, we were able to make some tea, which helped keep our spirits up. For this was the day when we would either succeed or fail. But we had come so far that we had no intention of failing now.

As daylight grew brighter we were able to take stock of our position. We were directly opposite a dock in which, laying alongside the jetty, were two big merchant ships, the *Alabama* and the *Portland*.

We were, in fact, right in the middle of a great deal of bustling activity. Across the river great winches clanked as the merchant ships were loaded. Beyond the reeds, only yards from where we were hidden, were houses and not far from them was a road from which came the constant roaring of cars and the occasional clatter of heavy military traffic. Shipping constantly passed us by up and down the river.

For the rest of the day we sat among the tall reeds, invisible to anyone ashore. We were relatively comfortable and able to talk in low whispers as well as smoke. We spent much of the day stretched out in the canoes asleep, conserving our strength for the coming evening. We were in good humour, delighted that we had penetrated so deep into enemy territory.

The day began to wane. As the light faded we had one more meal, the last we would have in our canoes. Then we took the limpet mines from beneath our legs and began the delicate job of fusing them, timing them to explode eight hours later; time enough to for us to make our getaway. Blondie then took the six-foot-long placing rod and made sure that it engaged and disengaged each mine. After that, he took us through our instructions one more time.

He and I would penetrate the main dock and attack whatever targets we found there. Laver and Mills were to keep to the north side of the river. If they found no targets, they were to return to attack the two merchant ships opposite. The job completed, we would paddle back downstream on the ebb tide as far as possible, until the next flood or the arrival of morning, then scuttle the canoes and head overland.

'Remember, Corporal,' he told Laver, 'when the job has been done, you and Mills must make your own way back. We cannot travel together. Good luck to you all.'

It was time to move.

We shook hands and wished each other the best of luck. I was especially sorry to say goodbye to Bill Mills who had been my close friend these past months. 'I'll get the first round when we return to Southsea,' I promised him.

The Corporal and Bill pulled away first. Blondie and I watched them slip across the river towards Bordeaux. Then we set off, paddling out far enough to find the tide that towed us along on our side of the river. It was an exhilarating moment; this was what we had been training for during those months of sweat and toil.

The going was easy with the flood tide carrying us onwards, perfect for the night's work; hopefully, there would be an ebb to help our escape. The rain had stopped; there was no wind and no clouds; the sky was clear and cold.

We approached the basin of Bordeaux. Lights shone from the jetties; so much illumination alarmed us. We paddled up the middle of the stream, inspecting the targets as we passed silently by. There were several ships moored in a row, which was very thoughtful of the Germans, making our targets so readily accessible. The first was a tanker. Next we found a cargo-liner. Then another cargo ship but with a tanker moored alongside. Then another cargo ship. Just beyond that we saw another ship which was impossible to identify because, lying alongside and obscuring our view, was a *sperrbrecher*, a smaller craft, no bigger than a frigate. We were lucky. We could have arrived to discover that the harbour was empty; there had been no way to knowing how many ships we would find until this moment, and we were satisfied. We chose four targets.

We turned back towards the cargo ship and pulled up alongside. Her hull shrouded us in darkness. We could hear the crew singing. I wondered what they'd be singing in a few hours' time. It proved an easy target. I attached my magnet-holder to the hull to prevent the tide from carrying us away. The Major placed the first mine on the six-foot rod and lowered it into the water, placing the mine on her stern. He detached the rod, having felt the limpet mine clamp itself to the hull. I released my magnetic holder and the tide slowly swept us along, so we could place another mine amidships and a third on her bows.

Then we came to the ship with the *sperrbrecher* moored to it. I clamped the holder to the hull and Blondie planted a mine.

Suddenly we were bathed in light. I looked up and saw the silhouette of a German sentry leaning over the side, shining his torch on us. We froze, hardly daring to breathe. A succession of split-second thoughts raced through my mind; what do we do if he challenges us? Do we answer? Just ignore him? If we ignore him, will he sound the alarm?

I quickly realized the best course of action was to hang onto the side of the ship. We were still well camouflaged, but the cockpit cover was open so I could hand Blondie the limpets. I cautiously leant forward, bending right across the cockpit so that my camouflaged back would conceal it. It may have been only seconds – it seemed like minutes – that we waited, but I began to think that we could sit there no longer. I gently eased the magnetic holder off, allowing the tide to carry us along the side of the ship.

But it wasn't enough to shake off the sentry. He walked along the deck, shining his torch on us. My main worry then was that the tide would carry us away from the ship; fortunately we stayed close to the hull. I could hear him grunting and I imagined him taking his rifle from his shoulder. My back felt naked. Any minute I expected to hear the bolt of his rifle, followed by a shot; it might be the last sound I ever heard.

We continued to drift, and he continued to follow. Gradually we drifted under the flare of the bows, out of his sight. I quickly reapplied my magnetic holder, clamping us firmly against the bows. We could see the beam of his torch searching the surface of the river. Then the light went off and we heard his hobnailed boots clanking away. If he had seen us, as he surely must, our camouflage must have been good enough to convince him we were nothing more than flotsam.

Blondie placed another mine on the bow. That'll teach him to upset us, I thought.

We turned to paddle back to our next target: the two ships tied up together. It seemed logical to attack both ships at the same time, so we eased our tiny craft between the two hulls, placing a mine on each stern. The Major also put a further mine on the cargo ship. He was just withdrawing his placing rod when, without warning, the tide began to bring the two ships together. We were caught in the middle.

We tried to free ourselves but were caught fast. The canoe began to crack, a muffled sound like pistols firing, as it was squeezed between the giant vessels. I thought that somebody was bound to hear and come looking. If we weren't finally crushed to death, we would certainly be discovered. In a desperate, futile move to save ourselves, we pushed against the hulls like Samson between the pillars of the temple.

It was luck and a change in the tide that saved us. The swell parted the ships, and we paddled away as fast as we could. Free from the danger, I wiped the sweat from my eyes. I had thought that I was going to die.

We had attacked three ships, placing eight mines. Our job was complete. Blondie and I shook hands and then made our way to midstream. Our timing was perfect; the tide had turned and was on the ebb. Paddling was easy and we made good speed out of the harbour, happy to leave it behind. We hoped to put as much distance between ourselves and the harbour as possible.

After we'd been paddling for a while, there came a splashing noise ahead of us. We stopped and sat in anxious silence, listening, peering into the dark. Then, a little way ahead, we made out the shape of another canoe. It was *Crayfish* with Laver and Mills. They had also heard us and had stopped, waiting to discover what was following them. They were as relieved as we were.

We pulled alongside and in a low voice Laver reported success. They found no target on the north side, so as the Major had told them they went back and attacked the two ships, putting five limpets on the first ship and three on the second.

'Well done,' Blondie said. We all exchanged congratulatory handshakes. It was a moment of sheer satisfaction. The job had been accomplished. We were all proud. Although very tired and cold, we were warmed a little as we basked for a few moments in our bit of glory.

'Well,' Blondie said. 'Nothing else now but to go our separate ways and make good our escape.'

'Funny,' Bill Mills remarked. 'It's my birthday today. I wish I could stay to hear the fireworks. Well, see you back at Portsmouth.'

I shook Bill's hand and told him I'd be home first to buy him a birthday drink.

'You two must continue on for another quarter of a mile,' Blondie told Laver and Mills. 'Then make your way across France as best you can. Good luck to you both.'

Then we all shook hands one last time. 'Don't forget your promise to buy the first round,' Bill said to me. Then he and Laver paddled away into the darkness. I wished so much that they could have stayed with us, but the Major was right: four men travelling together would look much more suspicious than two. He was, after all, the gov'nor.

That same night, as Laver, Mills, Blondie and I pulled out from the reeds to begin our attack on the ships at Bordeaux, Wallace and Ewart emerged from their interrogations. They were only a mile from our last hiding place. Despite all the Security Police inflicted on them, the two lads had said nothing of us. The Germans believed they had tortured all the information out of the prisoners.

Soon after midnight a member of the Security Police led them out into the town square where a truck awaited. They were accompanied by a doctor and a naval party of sixteen ratings, including Lieutenant Theodor Prahm, Adjutant to the naval officer in charge. Wallace and Ewart were thrown into the truck. The rest boarded other vehicles forming a small convoy which drove out of the square. Beyond the edge of the town they turned down a track and after a short bumpy ride the truck came to a halt. Wallace and Ewart were hustled out and in the light of the trucks' headlamps, turned full on, they found themselves in a sandpit with two posts driven into the sand.

The two Commandos were tied to the posts. Prahm shouted an order. The ratings stood to in a line. Another order. The firing squad raised their rifles, took aim and fired.

Only hours later, at 7.00am, an explosion ripped through the *Alabama*. It was only the first in a series of explosions to rock the ships docked at Bordeaux. At 8.30am the first of our own mines went off and within half an hour the rest had all exploded. The last of Corporal Laver's mines finally went off at 1.00pm. The French fire brigade arrived and apparently did their best to add to the damage.

The names of the ships have gone down in history merely because of the damage inflicted on them. The *Dresden* sank with holes in her outer plating and her propeller-shaft tunnel. The *Portland* was badly holed and damaged by fire. The *Tannenfels* was also badly holed, causing her to list severely. However, like the *Alabama* and *Portland* she was later patched up sufficiently by divers to be pumped out and put in dry dock for repairs. There were two other ships attacked; the damage sustained by them was not discovered.

I was sorry not to see the fireworks. But I had done my job — both for my country and for my brother, Benny.

5

THE TIDE HAD TURNED AGAINST US, making paddling heavy work. We paddled on briefly against the flood, then turned in towards the shore, not far from the village of St. Genés et Blaye, and came to ground in soft mud. We climbed out of the canoe, stretching our cramped legs and weary arms. Then we emptied the canoe, removing the few rations we still had left, plus a container of fresh water and spare clothes and boots. These things we could take, Blondie announced, but the Sten gun had to be disposed of — and despite my protest he hurled it out into the river. It was too cumbersome to carry, he said. At least we still had our fighting knives and Colt .45s, as well as a hand grenade.

Then Blondie turned his attention to the canoe itself, reminding me that we must leave no trace of our presence whatsoever. Like him I drew my knife and began to slash the boat's canvas sides. Now I know how a cowboy feels when he has to shoot his horse because it has broken its leg. That canoe had been a faithful friend, but here I was, hacking and slicing at it like a butcher cleaving through a side of beef.

Then, as I kept watch, peering into the darkness, Blondie pushed the canoe out into the river. He waded out until the water was up to his waist, trying to force the boat under. Gradually it filled up, rolled slightly and began to sink. I heard the remaining pockets of air bubbling up and, forgetting for a moment that I was supposed to be keeping a look out, turned to see the last of the canoe as it slid below the surface.

Blondie emerged from the water. 'Come on,' he said. 'We need to get out of these uniforms and find some other clothing.'

We set off towards dry land, trudging through the mud for some fifty yards until we came to a bank. It was six feet high and topped with thick reeds. We scrambled up, slipping and sliding, and snaked among the reeds. Stretched out before us lay a field, and beyond that a copse of bushes. We checked for signs of life but could detect none. Still watching and listening intently, we hurried across the field and flung ourselves down among the bushes. We were both exhausted.

It was still an hour or so till daylight, so Blondie decided we should rest up. Neither of us could have kept awake for much longer anyway. We didn't need to worry about sentry duty, for we were well hidden among the bushes. The night was cold but, oblivious to the frost settling on me, I was quickly asleep.

It was dawn when I woke, shivering, with stiff limbs, suddenly aware that I was frozen.

'Tea, Bill?'

Blondie was already awake and brewing tea. While my brain was screaming out, now that the job was done and the tension had eased, he had a new calmness about him. I sat up and took the hot cup. What was our next move, I asked.

'We're going to go home,' he replied.

'Yes, but *how* are we going to get home?'

Patiently he repeated what he had already explained. First we must go to Ruffec and make contact with an escape organization ...

'But what if we *don't* make contact? Suppose we don't get to Ruffec? And how are we going to get hold of some civilian clothes? What if ...?' Blondie remained unperturbed as I reeled off my list of 'What ifs'. He understood my worries. What I failed to realize was how anxious he was too. But then, he never showed it. He just allowed me to vent my feelings while never betraying his own fears and apprehensions. He was as keen to get home as I was, but he never did or said anything that for one single second suggested he had lost hope.

'We'll try and get a change of clothes and then we can travel by day,' he said. 'But not yet. First we must put as many miles behind us as possible. We're too close to the river to start knocking at doors and asking for help. We'll get going when you've finished your tea.'

Travelling by day at this stage was rather risky while we were still in uniform, but we couldn't afford to wait any longer in case the enemy managed to trace us to our landing place. As soon as I finished my tea, we set out on what we knew was going to be a long trek. It would take us about a week of walking to reach Ruffec.

After just a short distance we came across a wire fence, about three feet high. We stepped over it, walked on, and before long came to another fence, then another, and another. I grumbled that the French must be stupid, putting so many fences across their fields.

'You silly devil,' said Blondie.'They're to support the vines. These are vineyards.'

Well, what did I know about vineyards? Being a Cockney, I'd never seen such a thing before. I was to grow sick of the sight of them before the day was out, as we crossed fence after fence.

Dusk arrived and I prepared myself for what I supposed would be another long cold night under the stars. But Blondie thought we should rest up for only a couple of hours, and then continue walking through the night. If we kept only to daylight hours we were bound to get spotted in our uniforms.

We settled down behind some bushes and I quickly drifted off. Two hours later Blondie woke me. 'Time to get going,' he said.

Bleary-eyed, hungry and cold, I got to my feet, and on we went. At least being on the move kept me a bit warmer and, trekking across the fields under cover of darkness gave us a certain sense of security. After a short while we came to a road. Now we grew cautious again and drew back from the road, anxious that at the moment we crossed we might find ourselves caught in the headlights of a passing vehicle. We crept to the edge of the road, keeping low. There seemed to be nothing approaching from either direction.

'Looks okay,' said Blondie. 'Right, let's go.'

We shot across like greyhounds and dived into a hedge on the other side. Suddenly, glancing back, we caught sight of a cyclist passing the very spot where we had crossed. He was almost certain to have seen us. I reasoned that it might just be one of the locals.

Blondie shook his head. 'It's past curfew. He's probably a gendarme.'

'Well, that's all right then, sir. We were told we could rely on the gendarmes in a tight corner.' That was the information given to us by intelligence.

Blondie was doubtful, but at least the man did not appear to be turning back to look for us. We watched him pedal on and disappear round a bend. Hoping that would be the last we saw of him, we hurried on, crossing the next field until once more we found ourselves approaching a lane. Again we checked that each way was clear, then dashed across. And as we did we became aware of a cyclist coming down the lane. It might just have been a different man but such a coincidence made Blondie suspicious. Still, there wasn't much we could do except keep going and hope we lost him. Otherwise we would have to get rid of him permanently.

We crossed the next field and shortly came to yet another lane.

76

This time we took no chances. We kept hidden for a while, peering up and down the lane to check that no one, especially the cyclist, was coming along. Sure enough, there he was again.

'Nothing else for it,' Blondie said. 'We'll have to make sure he doesn't have the chance to give us away. We'll use our knives.'

We stepped back into the shadows and drew our knives. As we stood waiting for him to approach, I secretly prayed that he would just turn around and go away. I had never killed a man face to face before, yet here I was about to cold-bloodedly knife to death a man I had never seen before. It was a different proposition to placing mines on a ship or firing at someone from a distance with a machine gun. In those situations you don't see their faces, you can't touch them, they have no identity — they are just the *enemy*. The prospect turned me cold, but it had to be done. If he would just turn around and go back the way he came ...

And yet I wanted to know who he was. He might have been a gendarme. He might have been a German. He might even have been a farmer out breaking curfew. We would soon find out; I hoped he would be a German. Then I realized that whoever he was, someone would miss him if he didn't return and that might bring a patrol out looking for us. There was no alternative; the man had to die.

We held our breath and waited in the darkness of the bushes. He was close now, within several yards of us. We coiled up like springs. Just get the job done, I thought. Quickly and quietly. He must have no chance of shouting out.

Then, unexpectedly, for no obvious reason, he stopped. He stared into the darkness ahead as though looking for something — or sensing something. He just sat there, perched on his bike. My hand was warm and wet about the handle of my knife as I brought it up, ready to plunge it into his chest. My mouth was dry and my heart thumped double quick time against my ribs. What was he waiting for?

It seemed like ages before he finally turned around and began to pedal off into the night. Maybe he had heard us. Maybe he had decided he had pursued us for long enough. Maybe he had a sixth sense that he was within seconds of death. Why he decided to turn back, we would never know. But he probably never knew how lucky he was to escape with his life.

We waited for several minutes to ensure he had not discovered a new burst of courage that would bring him back. Finally, satisfied that he was no longer a menace but checking once more that the coast was clear, we crossed the road and continued over the fields.

We rested up occasionally but otherwise walked through the night and into the early hours of the morning of 13 December. When dawn came we were overlooking a valley with a lonely farmhouse nestling on the lower slopes.

The time had come to try our luck, Blondie decided. We might be able to get some clothes here. He told me to wait while he went down first to see if they were friendly. If he didn't return within a quarter of an hour, I was to get away from the area as fast as possible. I didn't like the idea of leaving the Major under any circumstances, but he was adamant.

I watched him make his way cautiously down the hill. For the first time since the operation had begun, I suddenly felt strangely alone. He went to the farmhouse door and knocked. It opened and he went inside. A few minutes later he reappeared and signalled me to join him.

I hurried down to the house, all the time looking about to make sure there was no one to see me. As I stepped through the door I was met by a stout, middle-aged woman and her husband, a small wiry farmer. There was also an old woman, probably the farmer's mother-in-law, and several children. On all their faces was trepidation and doubt, even fear; obviously they were suspicious of two men who had turned up out of the blue, claiming to be English Commandos. For all they knew we could be Germans. We had put them in some danger for they could be shot if they were found to be harbouring us.

The farmer's wife glared at me. Then she spoke.

'She says you are young, that you shouldn't be a soldier at all,' Blondie explained with a grin.

Too young, I thought. Bloody cheek! How old did she think I was?

Then Blondie turned to our host and seemed to be pleading with him. I knew he must be asking for clothing and a little food. The farmer had a muttered discussion with his wife, then said something which the Major translated for me. They had no food to spare but could give us clothes.

Blondie expressed his gratitude but they wanted no thanks; just for us to leave. We could sense that they still had doubts about us, probably fearful that if we were Germans they would be arrested. They gave us each a pair of rough overall trousers and I also got a poacher's jacket. They had no spare shoes but our commando boots would not be too obvious.

The Major told them to burn our uniforms; it was as important for themselves as it was for us. If the Germans should come looking, it was essential they did not find our uniforms. The farmer nodded his understanding but his wife was already trying to get rid of us, almost pushing us out of the door.

Again Blondie thanked them. We knew these people were risking their lives for us. As we said our goodbyes he added: 'The day of liberation is getting closer.'

This news did not placate them. They were only relieved to see us go. Poor buggers, I thought; they'd probably be on edge all day, worrying that we might have been the enemy after all and that soldiers might come to arrest them.

We had only just left the farm when the Major said something that really alarmed me. 'We'll have to discard the rest of our arms. If we're found in civilian clothes and armed, it will be the firing squad for certain.'

I didn't like it at all as we relieved ourselves of our pistols, knives and hand grenade. Now we were defenceless. I understood the Major's reasoning, but I always liked to feel I was capable of defending myself if the need arose.

In civilian clothes we could travel by day. But it was very unnerving all the same, walking openly along the road, being passed by a great deal of traffic, much of it military.

'Just keep calm,' Blondie told me. 'Imagine we're out for a nice walk. Don't look concerned.'

With all those bloody Germans around I found this harder to do than expected! Every now and then a German lorry passed by. Some lorries carried troops who looked out at us, and we had to behave as though we weren't in the slightest bit interested. The last thing we wanted was to draw attention to ourselves. We just ignored them while at the back of my neck my hair was standing on end. Suppose one of them shouts something out and expects a reply, I kept thinking. Or suppose they stop and come and question us?

Each time a military truck passed and disappeared into the distance, I heaved a sigh of relief, but Blondie never so much as flinched. He chatted away to me in French, gesticulating wildly the way Frenchmen do, while I nodded agreeably or shrugged my shoulders, not having understood a word.

'What do I do if we are stopped?' I asked.

'Say nothing,' said Blondie. 'Pretend you are mute.'

Two days earlier, shortly after we had all shaken hands and said our goodbyes, Corporal Laver and Bill Mills had paddled on down the river, putting a quarter of a mile between themselves and us. When they pulled into shore they were just beyond Blaye. They scuttled their canoe and took off on foot. They made good progress, covering some fifteen or twenty miles, bringing them two days later to La Garde, a town that was just twelve miles from a hamlet called Villexavier through which, on that very day, the Major and I were passing. It was 14 December.

Unlike the Major and myself, Laver and Mills had not been able to get hold of civilian clothes and therefore had to stick to walking only in the dark and avoiding all roads. Their only hope was to skirt around La Garde. Exactly what happened we have no way of knowing. Maybe they made the mistake of believing that the gendarmes were, as British Intelligence had reported, on our side, and consequently approached a French police officer who immediately had them placed under arrest. Whatever the circumstances the gendarmes took them prisoner and handed them over to the Germans. They were taken to Security Police headquarters at Bordeaux for interrogation.

The Germans would later name Laver and Mills as members of the Commando unit, along with Wallace and Ewart, that had attacked shipping in Bordeaux. The report claimed that they wore no military badges, an evil lie concocted by the Germans to justify their execution of Wallace and Ewart which was clearly against international law. With this lie they intended that Laver and Mills should meet the same fate.

Following their interrogation, they were taken to Paris for further questioning.

The village of St Mème-les-Carrières lay ahead of us. Intelligence had assured us it was not occupied by German troops, otherwise we would have given it a wide berth for sure. As it was, we continued along the road and walked straight into the village.

Suddenly there came the call of a bugle — a military bugle. We froze, mystified and startled, looking all around for any sign of soldiers. More cautiously we moved on, passing a large old house. As we drew abreast of it the door flew open and out stampeded a whole troop of German soldiers. To them it didn't matter that we were directly in their path. They thrust past us, shoving and pushing us, almost knocking us down. My normal reaction would have been to swear loudly and push back, but I checked myself, knowing that this would be fatal. More men spilled out of the door and barged into us, knocking the wind out of us. We fought down the urge to retaliate. All we could do was struggle to keep our feet. They seemed to take delight in buffeting us to and fro; but, angry as was, I continued to hold back. I was more frightened than mad.

And then they were gone, running off down the road, laughing and joking, having enjoyed their sport; some thirty German soldiers, any of whom could have been the one to discover the whereabouts of the saboteurs of Bordeaux.

We were both shaken by the experience and indescribably relieved. Without a word we carried on walking, eager to leave the hamlet behind.

By now we were getting very hungry but our rations were all used up and we began to consider where our next meal was coming from. Blondie summed up our options: we could either knock at a remote farmhouse and ask for food, or we could just steal some.

Just then we saw a freshly ploughed field ahead of us. We had been trained to scavenge for food so it was not a difficult decision to leave the road and take whatever bounty the farmworkers had left behind. To our delight we discovered potatoes and turnips and soon we had gathered a small harvest. We had no way of cooking them, however, so they had to be eaten raw. Our escape packs included special tablets that helped us to digest raw vegetables. The trouble was that I liked the taste of these tablets and had taken to nibbling mine from time to time. In fact I had eaten them all. I was counting on Blondie's generosity. He was never one to be selfish.

'Well,' he said now, 'you're not getting any of mine.' And he was as good as his word.

We ate as we walked. Further down the road we came across a farmer who was shouting at his horse. I turned to Blondie and said quietly, 'Stupid man, shouting at his horse. It's just a dumb animal.'

'That horse is more intelligent than you,' replied Blondie. 'At least he can understand French.'

As well as dry humour, he also possessed an incredible abundance of patience. I often reached a point of such frustration that I would loose off with a long succession of complaints.

'But for you, I'd be back in Portsmouth now,' I'd tell him.

'Instead here we are, lost in France. What are we going to do? How are we ever going to get home?'

He never admonished me for it. He just waited for the storm to abate and calmly said, 'Have you finished?'

Darkness approached and we began to look around for somewhere to spend the night. Off the road we discovered a densely wooded area and decided it would be a safe haven for the night. Hidden among the trees we were able to brew up some tea.

It was still bitterly cold, especially in the morning. I took out my flask of Pusser's Rum and treated myself to a tot. Even though Blondie had not shared his tablets with me, I couldn't let him go without a drop of rum, too; but it wasn't enough to warm us through thoroughly and our stomachs were once again empty.

We marched on once more, resting up occasionally and keeping a look-out for further fields of turnips or potatoes or anything else we could eat. But by the time dusk began to fall we had found none. We were still some twenty-one miles from Ruffec. Blondie reckoned it was time to trust to luck and knock on a door somewhere.

Just before it grew too dark, we came across an isolated farmhouse. We bided our time, remaining at a distance for quite a while, keeping the house under surveillance. We saw nobody leave or enter and, deciding it was as safe a place as any we might find, we made our way towards the house. Blondie knocked on the door.

It was answered by a middle-aged lady. As the Major launched into his usual French patter, her face darkened and yelling something at him she slammed the door in our faces.

'Quick, let's get away from here,' Blondie said and we scurried off. I was totally bewildered, as I'm sure he was.

'I thought these people were supposed to be on our side,' I grumbled. 'Here we are helping these people out, we've just done a job to help their country, risking our lives, and they don't want to know us. Is all this worth it?'

I was feeling really miserable. From the time we had been seen by the fisherfolk on our way to Bordeaux, we had been met with suspicion by the French. I just couldn't figure it out. Nor could the Major. It would be some weeks before we discovered the cause.

Concerned that the French woman might give us away, we hurried on down the lane, no longer feeling inclined to knock on any doors. Then it began to rain. Our priority now was to find somewhere dry for the night.

We came across a track that left the lane and led to a row of several houses. What really attracted our attention, though, was a large barn. The rain was falling heavily now, soaking us through to the skin. We set off down the track until we came to the barn, stepped cautiously inside and were relieved to find it empty. There was nothing to hand to satisfy our hunger but at least we would be warm and dry.

We settled down in the hay; it felt like luxury, certainly the best accommodation we'd had since the submarine. I lay there feeling that maybe things were looking up at last. I drifted off into a sleep, unconcerned with the world.

I sat bolt upright, suddenly awake. A light was being shone right in my face. I leapt to my feet, reaching for my pistol and suddenly remembering it was no longer there. Now I wished that I had disobeyed the Major and kept my weapons. I was prepared to make a fight of it.

The man with the torch was a farmer. The Major was up on his feet and giving his usual 'Hello, we are English Commandos ...' routine.

'It is dangerous here,' the farmer said. 'The people who live here do not want you here. It is lucky I saw you or the Boche might come for you. Come with me to my house and I will give you some food.'

When Blondie had translated I needed no persuasion. I was ravenous. But to Blondie it wasn't that easy. He wanted to be sure that this was not a trap, and he kept the conversation going until he felt that, at the very least, we had no other course but to trust the farmer. We followed him outside. The rain was still pouring but it was just a short walk along the track to his house.

We stepped inside. The place was cheered by a blazing log fire. 'Sit, sit,' the farmer said. 'Warm yourselves.'

We sat by the crackling fire, basking in the warmth while the farmer disappeared into the kitchen. He soon came back with some soup and bread for us. We could not sleep in the house, the farmer told Blondie, but we were welcome to spend the night in his cow shed. It would be warmer there than in the barn, and if someone had seen us entering the barn it would be unwise to return there.

We finished eating and followed the farmer back out into the rain. The cow shed was close by. Inside it was dry and a lot less draughty than the barn. Warning us not to go outside for anything in case we were seen, and wishing us goodnight, the farmer went back to his house.

Blondie and I snuggled down in the hay. I was still soaked but the warm dry hay was immediately comforting and luxurious. I lay back and waited for sleep to come.

I had just dropped off when I became aware of someone leaning over the Major and grabbing him. I shot up, but realized it was the farmer.

Somebody had seen us. The gendarmes were on their way. The farmer shooed us out with urgent warnings to avoid the road and keep to the track instead. As we snatched up our few possessions and scrambled towards the door the frantic farmer was virtually pushing us towards the window. It was too dangerous to go out through the door, he told Blondie, so we had to use the window.

We climbed out of the window and ran as fast as we could down the narrow, muddy track. The rain was fierce. I was miserable at being denied such a nice warm place to rest up for the night.

'What is it with these people?' I complained. 'Why do they want to turn us in?'

Blondie was his usual calm and understanding self. 'Something must have happened to make them all frightened,' he said. 'It's possible that if we were found by the Germans in that village, everyone there would suffer.'

He turned out to be correct, for the Germans had found imprints of our boots in the mud along the river, and then published the prints in the newspapers, making it clear that anyone who saw such impressions in the ground should report it immediately.

With rain squelching in our boots, we reached the top of the lane and turned to look back in time to see a party of gendarmes searching for us. We turned into a field.

'Wait,' Blondie said. 'Getting away from here as fast as we can is just what they will be expecting us to do. Our best bet is to get under a good thick hedge and wait until morning before making a move.'

This sounded like good reasoning to me. We picked a suitable hedge and eased ourselves under it. There we lay, with the bush offering little shelter from the rain that cascaded down the branches and leaves and ran like streams down our faces. I closed my eyes, trying to fall asleep. Eventually I managed to slip into unconsciousness.

It had stopped raining by the time daylight broke. All was quiet. We emerged cautiously from our hiding place. We were thoroughly cold and wet, but still free and alive. All about us, nothing stirred.

We set off, and shortly found the road again. We had evaded capture by the seats of our borrowed pants, and I looked forward to getting home and finding the person in Intelligence who had said that the gendarmes were on our side. Although we didn't feel safe yet, we did feel that the immediate danger had passed. Our only fear was that the farmer who had helped us might get into trouble. But there was nothing we could do. We had to keep going. It was 18 December.

The rest of the day was, thankfully, uneventful. We started off with food in our stomachs from the night before, but by nightfall we were hungry again. We decided it was worth risking knocking at another door.

We found a suitable looking house, this time one that was remote, void of any nosy neighbours to worry us. It stood on the edge of a forest; perfect, if we had to make a quick getaway. We waited a while to ensure the coast was clear, then stepped up to the front door and knocked.

A young girl answered; she looked no older than fifteen. Blondie asked to speak to her mother, but she said her mother did not live here; she was the woman of the house. For once, Blondie was taken by surprise, but he quickly recovered and came out with the familiar speech. 'We are English Commandos, and we need some food.'

She looked from Blondie to me and back again. Was this going to be another slammed door? Then she spoke; she was inviting us in.

We entered, relieved and grateful. But once inside we began to think that we had picked the wrong house to come begging at. The place had little furniture, although it was spotlessly clean. In a corner lay a small baby. I looked about, realizing how poor this young mother was.

'How can we ask her for any food?' I said to Blondie. 'She's probably got barely enough for herself.'

We were just wondering what to do next when the front door opened. In stepped a young man, barely sixteen. Yet despite his youth he looked every inch a roughneck and his first words were far from friendly. Obviously he was asking who we were and what we were doing in his house.

'We are English Commandos,' the Major said. I thought: We're going to get the old heave-ho, I'll bet.

The young man's face suddenly lit up. 'Ah, English Commandos!' He was genuinely pleased to see us.

Blondie explained that we were in France because we'd had a job to do and now we needed help to get back to England — and food.

The French lad was deeply interested in what Blondie had to say. He told us he would be glad to help us if he could, but he was not in a position to do very much. However, he had friends who could help, and he would take us to them.

We had no choice but to follow. Although he seemed genuine enough, there was still the risk that we could be led into a trap. We followed him through the forest and after about half an hour we spied, in a clearing, a little house, snugly hidden. It was, I thought, a little too secluded if we should happen to find ourselves among enemies. I felt uneasy. We had no way of knowing what this young man was leading us into.

We entered the house and found several of the most villainous looking Frenchmen I had ever seen. I was sure we were in for some trouble. Then we learned they were from a Maquis group; their intent was to kill Germans. We were among friends after all.

The lad introduced us to the leader of this group, a real tough-looking man who seemed unimpressed by the Major's explanation of who we were and what we were doing there. He began firing questions at me. I didn't understand a word so I just shrugged my shoulders. But their aggressive manner was not lost on me.

They soon turned their attention once more on Blondie. They continually pressed him for information about ourselves, and he told them the little that he could. They grew ever more loud and threatening. I began to think that we would be lucky to escape without getting our throats cut. I couldn't understand why they were so hostile; it was the Germans they should have been attacking, not us.

They suspected that we were in fact Germans out to discover their set-up. What still baffled me was why these, and all the other French people Blondie had spoken to, found it so difficult to believe we were English. Again I wished I had my pistol with me.

One of the men went behind a curtain and turned on a radio. From it came the voice of an English broadcaster, reporting the progress of our lads in North Africa. I lost interest in what was going on between Blondie and the other men, and began listening intently to the news.

I hadn't realized how closely the men were watching me. My face must have told the story better that the Major's French ever could.

'Your friend is pleased to hear the news,' they told Blondie, and their attitude suddenly changed.

'Our brave English friends,' they bellowed merrily. 'You must be hungry. We will bring you some food straight away.'

I didn't know what they were saying , but I could tell they were now satisfied. The simple fact that I had listened to that broadcast and my reactions towards it had convinced them we were not Germans. I had unwittingly saved our lives. At last we were safe — for the time being, anyway.

6

THE FRENCH ROUGHNECKS OF THE MAQUIS were suddenly our greatest friends. The man who owned the house now became a most gracious host, and he lavished bread, beans and ham on us. We could spend the night there; in fact, he insisted that we should.

There was a much older man there who decided to strike up a conversation with me. I turned to Blondie. 'What's he saying?'

'He wants to give you a drink.'

This was a cheery invitation indeed. I smiled broadly and in my best French accent, which left much to be desired, I said, 'Ah, oui!' which was about all the French I could manage. The man beckoned me to follow him. We went outside to a shed where he produced a bottle of brandy and a glass. He poured out a small amount for me. It was brilliant green but hardly more than a mouthful. Mean old bugger, is this all he's giving me, I thought.

I tipped it back, and gasped for breath; it nearly blew my head off. He laughed loudly as I clutched my burning throat. Right, I thought, I'll get my own back. 'Have a go at this, chum,' I said, taking out my flask of pusser's rum and offering it to him. He took the flask, put it to his lips and gulped greedily. When he finally stopped and handed the flask back to me, I tipped it upside down; not a drop fell out.

'You drank the lot,' I said. 'You *are* a mean old bugger!'

Later our host led us to a bedroom where we would spend the night. We realized that we were turning both him and his wife out of their own bed. Blondie protested that this was not necessary, but again the man was insistent. Not wanting to offend him, not now that he was on our side, we turned in for the night. I looked in wonder at the bed — a real bed. I tested it for comfort with my hand. Hard as a rock by normal standards, to me it felt like a bed of air. I lay down; Blondie climbed in beside me. That night we slept as soundly as two newborn babes.

Our host clattered into the room bright and early the next morning.

At the unveiling of the Special Boat Squadron memorial, Poole, 1982.

At the unveiling of a plaque at St Nicholas Church, Bordeaux. Mary Lindell is on Colonel Hasler's right.

On a promotional tour of the United States for the film of Cockleshell Heroes.

Colonel Hasler and the author revisit Bordeaux, 1966.

We rose, feeling refreshed and optimistic. Breakfast was ready, there was food to take with us and our water cans had been filled.

The young guide from the previous day had returned. He would show us where to go, he announced cheerfully, and tomorrow we should be in Ruffec.

Blondie thanked our host profusely and feeling as though we might really now be on our way to freedom, and with food in our bellies, we set off through the forest with the young man.

We made good headway and the day was thankfully void of any excitement. The time came for a brief respite. We sat down and took out our water cans for a refreshing drink. To my surprise and delight, instead of cool water I tasted a fruity red wine. Blondie, too, had been supplied with our host's very best wine. We decided we could get used to this, and took a few more gulps.

Our rest over, we carried on, but soon Blondie and I found that our legs were suddenly heavier. All I wanted to do was lie down and go to sleep.

'It's the wine,' said Blondie.

We had come to a stream and we emptied one of the cans and then refilled it with water. But we did keep the wine in the other can. The water helped to clear our heads, and we continued until evening when we came across a derelict barn.

There was no comfortable hay inside and the place was crawling with rats, but it offered us shelter for the night. We settled down on the concrete floor. I certainly missed our bed of the previous night, even if our host's wife had been forced to sleep elsewhere.

By this time we had used up all our tea, and my rum was gone, but we made do with the wine. It not only quenched our thirst but helped to induce sleep. The floor was cold and hard and the pitter-patter of rats make my skin crawl; but, thanks to the wine, I soon drifted off.

When I awoke in the morning, my thoughts were immediately about how we would soon be among friends and sleeping in a comfortable bed somewhere in Ruffec. Our mission to blow up shipping in Bordeaux now seemed years behind us and the real prospect of getting back home elated me. We set off eagerly on the last leg of this particular journey. Cutting across country, often trudging along flooded tracks that were ankle-deep from the recent downpours, we passed through the village of Rais. Like so many of the sleepy French villages, it seemed not to know that the rest of the world was at war. And few people paid any attention to three men passing through late in the morning, two of whom, Blondie and myself, were spattered with mud. We were tired by now and our clothes — and bodies — were beginning to smell stale.

Only three more miles to go, the guide told us.

This helped us to pick up the pace, and we tramped on across country for another two miles until, around midday, we came to another village, La Faye. There we picked up the main road and turned east. Another mile down the road, Ruffec came into sight. It looked as if our days of hiking all over the country were about at an end.

This was where the young man had to leave us. With smiles and waves he brushed off our thanks. 'Bonne chance,' he said. And with that he turned and doubled back on his trail.

Our instructions now were to find the Café de Paris in Ruffec where we could expect further help, so we set off briskly and soon found ourselves in the little town. We hoped that we looked like any other Frenchmen but we were in something of a state with mud caked to our clothes. We knew there was a large detachment of soldiers occupying the town, and kept alert, but strangely enough we saw very few. Maybe they were having a dose of fatigues, I muttered to myself.

We walked one street after another, looking for the Café de Paris but without success. Trying to appear casual, we stopped to look in shop windows to give ourselves a moment or two to assess our situation which was beginning to look hopeless. We had covered virtually every square foot of the town and checked out every bistro, I grumbled at the Major. 'But no Café de bloody Paris.'

He was beginning to worry that people might get suspicious about the two strangers walking around. He decided we should enter the first suitable bistro and wait there in the hope that someone from the escape organization would come looking for us. We had 2,000 francs in our escape kit which was enough to buy ourselves a decent meal.

We found what we thought would be as good a café as any to take refuge in. Looking through the window, pretending to study the menu, we counted about a dozen customers inside. We entered and sat down at a table. A very ample woman came over to take our order. Naturally, I left it to Blondie to choose for me. But then she said something that turned his face pale.

Everything was rationed. We needed ration cards, even for coffee. We had no ration cards, of course. The woman was looking at us very suspiciously.

I could see the alarm mounting on Blondie's face. Then the woman seemed to relent. Apparently potato soup was not rationed, so Blondie ordered two potato soups.

She left and Blondie explained to me the situation in a whisper. 'At least the soup will be hot and filling,' he said, 'and it'll help us to pass time here while we wait.'

'Yes,' I said, 'but wait for what?'

'Hopefully for our helpers to come looking for us.'

My fear was that it was the Germans who would come looking for us. There was no way of knowing if Madame had more in mind for us than potato soup.

She returned with the soup. It was thick with vegetables and very tasty. We tried to make it last, but eventually our bowls were empty and still nobody had come in and approached us, friendly or otherwise.

Blondie ordered some more soup. Then, when we had finished our second helpings, he decided there was nothing else for it but to have a third course. By this time the few remaining customers were watching us. Any of them could have been a German out of uniform. I began to wish I had my weapons again.

'It looks as though we're on our own,' Blondie finally said.

Quietly he told me he was going to take a risk and see if the woman would help us. After all, we had little choice. We would never make it to Spain on our own. In his schoolboy French he wrote a short note: '*We are escaping English soldiers. Do you know anyone who can help?*'

He beckoned Madame over to pay the bill, and passed her the bill along with a 500-franc note. She went back to the till and discovered, wrapped inside the bill, his note. She unfolded it and began to read. We watched with pained anxiety, knowing that if she was a German sympathizer it was too late now to do anything about it.

She visibly stiffened, folded the note, stuffed it away and began clearing the bistro of all the other customers. We remained at our table as she locked the door and, without a word to us, hurried out through the back door.

'She's gone for the Germans,' I said. 'I just know it.'

But Blondie stayed calm. Besides, as he pointed out, where could we run?

A short while later she came back in. I jumped, expecting a troop of Germans to come barging in after her, but the only person she brought was a little old man. And, to our astonishment, he said in perfect English, 'Who were you told to contact?'

'We were only told that friends of England would be here to help us,' the Major explained.

'Why did you come in here?'

'We had nowhere else to go and we were hungry.'

'What were you doing in this country?'

'We've had a job to do and now we are trying to get back home.'

The old man persisted. 'What kind of a job?' It was a loaded question. If this man was a German agent, he was the last person we would want to tell.

'I can't tell you that, I'm afraid.'

His response stunned us. 'Was it in Bordeaux?'

'It may have been near Bordeaux.'

The old man then explained to Madame what had been said. To us he said, 'I wish I could help you, but there is nothing I can do for you. I wish you good luck.' Then he left.

I was still nursing bitter disappointment when, moments later, a younger man entered. He asked the same questions, only in French. Blondie gave his answers.

'I cannot help you,' said the Frenchman at last. 'The town is crawling with the Boche.' Then he left, too. At least the word 'Boche' suggested that we were among friends. Or were these people just stalling for time? We wondered how many more were going to come and question us and yet offer no help.

Blondie asked Madame if she could give us a room for the night. She nodded and led us upstairs. The room had what we craved — a proper bed. Then she disappeared, returning a few minutes later with a small bath. She also brought a towel, a bar of soap and a bucket of hot water. As soon as she had gone, we stripped naked and gave ourselves a good wash all over. It felt good to be clean again.

We sat back on the bed, discussing where we should go next. The feel of the mattress beneath me was inviting. I felt overwhelmingly tired.

'We'll just have to wait and see what tomorrow brings,' Blondie said, yawning.

I snuggled down. 'So long as it doesn't bring the Germans.' My eyes began to close.

'Well, we can hardly fight our way out stark naked,' Blondie mumbled.

Then we both succumbed.

After what seemed like only moments we were rudely shaken out of our sleep by a loud knock at the door. We looked at each other in horror.

'Germans!' I said.

'Go and see,' Blondie said.

'Why me?'

'Because I'm a Major.'

I got out of bed, struggled into my trousers and went to the door. I hesitated to open it. Another loud knock. There was nothing for it but to open the door. To my amazement there stood, not a German stormtrooper, but a little old lady. In perfect English she said, 'Can I come in?'

She told us she had just come to bring us some chocolate and have a little chat. I was in no mood for any more talk, so I left it to the Major, sitting naked in bed, to play host to this latest interrogator.

As I half listened to their conversation, I began to notice how she seemed to be fencing with the Major, as though she was trying to catch him out. I grew suspicious of her.

Eventually she said, 'Well, I must go. I wish you both good luck.' She went to the door, turned and told us to be ready to leave in an hour. A van would come for us and take us to the line of demarcation. With that, she left. She was indeed an agent for the French Resistance.

The demarcation line was the border through the middle of France that had separated the occupied half of the country from the unoccupied part. Many French people had escaped to the unoccupied part; but when the Germans later took over the whole of the country they set up the demarcation line to prevent escapees from returning to their original homes. It was heavily patrolled, and we would have to cross it.

The surprise news brought by the old lady startled us out of our tiredness and we readied ourselves to leave. At dusk there came a knock at the door. There stood our guide, a middle-aged man with a weasel face. I didn't like the look of him at all. I was still baffled by the repeated questioning we had undergone since our arrival, and couldn't help but remain suspicious that these people might in fact be about to turn us in.

Weasel Face led us downstairs to where Madame was waiting. Blondie thanked her warmly and she wished us 'bonne chance'. Then we went out the back way and straight into a waiting van. Again I was concerned, especially when I discovered that there was not even a single window for us to look out of. Weasel Face climbed into the cab and we drove off. Within minutes we had left Ruffec behind. Although we were now in the hands of the Resistance — *if* we were in the hands of the Resistance — we were still very much in danger, for the Germans were unceasingly hunting out escape organizations and there was no mercy for anyone found involved.

We came to a stop about twelve miles from Ruffec. We sat, waiting for the driver to open the back door for us. I had a vision of German soldiers waiting outside for us, and my pulse began to race as I heard the click of the door handle being turned. The door swung open. There stood Weasel Face.

We climbed down and found ourselves standing in long grass. It was dark and we appeared to be alone. I began to breathe more easily. We were told to wait here; someone would arrive later to lead us across the line of demarcation and to a place of safety. We should not move from this spot. We should not smoke. We should keep quiet as there were patrols about and they had dogs.

He got back into the van and drove away. We were on our own again but I was relieved to see the back of him. I was still not sure if he or the others could be trusted. The Germans were known to play elaborate games, infiltrating escape organizations and springing nasty surprises both on members of the organization and on escapees. But for the time being Blondie suggested that we should do as he'd said: sit and wait.

We were alert to any sound but we heard nothing. The minutes passed uneasily. Then an hour passed, or maybe two. Suddenly, as if from nowhere, a figure appeared out of the dark. We were taken by surprise. We were unarmed but prepared to defend ourselves with our fists and feet if necessary. Fortunately, it wasn't.

He was a short man and, more importantly, alone. He seemed genuinely pleased to see us, shaking us each vigorously by the hand.

We should follow him, he said. The line of demarcation was just ahead: a long main road which we had to cross. He would cross first, and if the coast was clear he'd give a whistle for one of us to follow. Then he'd whistle again when it was safe for the other to cross.

He disappeared as noiselessly as he had come.

The Major told me that he'd go next. The Germans might be watching. If they saw the Frenchman they might decide to wait for the next person with their machine gun ready. If I heard any firing, he said, I would have to go back.

There came the sound of a whistle. Blondie was off like a rabbit into the darkness. I waited, impatient for the signal and hoping there would be no gun fire. I hated to think that I should have to leave the Major, after all we'd gone through together. And besides, where would I go? I was torn between obeying orders and friendship.

I was thankful not to have to make a decision, for I heard the whistle. I took off, sprinting and jumping through the long grass and coming suddenly upon the road. I didn't stop to check if all was clear; that was the Frenchman's job. I flew across the road and found the Frenchman and Blondie waiting for me in some bushes.

'Well done, Bill,' said Blondie.

But already the Frenchman was setting off towards a forest and beckoning us to follow. We moved swiftly in and out of the trees, following no clearly marked trail. After about half an hour we saw the outline of a small farmhouse through the trees. We walked silently towards it. The only sound was that of animals in the outhouses. We reached the door and the guide knocked.

A young farmer opened the door and we were ushered in. This was Monsieur DuBois, said the guide; he would be our host for the next few days. Then bidding us 'bonne chance' he was gone, leaving us alone with the farmer and his family. As well as his wife and young baby, he also had his mother-in-law living in the house, as was typical of the French.

Monsieur DuBois seemed very keen to make us welcome. His wife brought us a meal and then we were shown to our room. It was on the ground floor, connected by a door to the living room, and contained a double bed, a table, a couple of chairs and a washbasin. Our host brought us in some books, both English and French, and a change of clothes.

We would have to remain in our room, he told us, but we still had to be careful. Outside of the room ran a public track and people might see us. We probably would not be here for too long, however, as the leader of the escape organization had been informed of our arrival and someone would come to collect us in a few days.

What organization was this, the Major wanted to know. Even he, I think, harboured some suspicions that we might still be in danger of being betrayed.

It was run by a British lady, Monsieur DuBois explained. They knew her as Marie-Claire.

When Blondie told me about this I was doubtful. I did not feel too happy about leaving my fate in the hands of a woman. But in time I would come to realize that Marie-Claire (her real name was Mary Lindell) was one of the most extraordinary and courageous people I could ever hope to meet.

Monsieur Louis Jaubert looked out of his window and was surprised to see his neighbour, Monsieur Cheyrau, walking along the railway track that ran close to his house. With Monsieur Cheyrau were two strangers, one wearing a blue serge suit and clearly suffering from a sore leg. In the village of Cessac, about twenty miles from Bordeaux, few strangers came. Monsieur Jaubert wondered if the men might be on the run from the Germans.

He left the window, opened his front door and went outside. Approaching his neighbour, he greeted him and asked who his friends were. Monsieur Cheyrau knew that his neighbour hated the Boche, so he told him: they were two Englishmen coming from Bordeaux.

Lieutenant Mackinnon and James Conway had understood not a word so far, but were heartened when Monsieur Jaubert spoke to them in English, inviting them to his home to share a bottle of wine. They were glad to accept and followed him to his home. There they met Madame Jaubert who, while courteous, was not as sure as her husband that these were genuine Englishmen. Nevertheless, she brought them wine, bread and thick vegetable soup. Mackinnon and Conway had not eaten so well in days.

Just what had happened between the time their canoe capsized and their discovery by Monsieur Jaubert is not known. But here they were, just a few days before Christmas, having avoided capture by the Germans and finding themselves among friends.

When Mackinnon expressed his gratitude, Monsieur Jaubert told him he was glad to help. He had a son in the army, he went on proudly. He had been evacuated from Dunkirk and hospitalized in England, where people treated him very well; but his only thought was to return to France and when he was discharged from hospital he came back.

'Where is he now?' Mackinnon asked.

Monsieur looked at Madame mournfully. 'He was taken prisoner by the Germans. But we hope to see him again — one day.'

Madame Jaubert had noticed Mackinnon's limp and demanded to see his leg. He rolled up his trouser to reveal a huge boil on his knee. Madame Jaubert cleaned it and dressed it with care while her husband tried to persuade the two men to stay. They thanked him but explained they were eager to move on, to meet someone who would help them escape.

'Then I will take you to the next village, Frontenac. I believe that members of escape organizations sometimes meet in cafés, and we may find someone.'

Despite his sore leg, Mackinnon was keen to get going, so the Frenchman immediately led the Englishmen to the neighbouring village of Frontenac, searching the cafés for anyone who might possibly be a member of an escape organization. But they found no one and returned to the Frenchman's house. There Madame Jaubert took their clothes and washed them, and was relieved to discover that their underpants had an English trademark on them. Now she knew for sure they really were English.

They were eventually making for Bilbao in Spain, Mackinnon explained to Monsieur Jaubert, but first they needed to go to Toulouse. He told them their best bet was to catch the train from La Réole; but it was a long way and they'd have to cross the line of demarcation. He would try and find someone who could help them across.

In the three days that followed, the Jauberts came to look upon the English lads with something close to parental affection. Then Monsieur found a guide willing to take the Commandos to La Réole.

There was a walk of some twenty-five miles ahead of them. It was time for them to go.

Madame Jaubert gave them a good supply of food. 'You come back to us after the war,' she said, and began to cry.

As the Jauberts hugged each of the Englishmen, Monsieur too shed some tears. Then they said their final goodbyes and Mackinnon and Conway went off down the road towards La Réole.

We awoke late after our first night at the farmhouse. It seemed peculiar to be sharing a double bed with the Major, but it was something I was to get used to.

Madame DuBois brought hot water into our room and we shaved and washed. By then she had returned with coffee, home-made bread, butter and jam. We were obviously going to be well cared for. Then I went outside to get some fresh air and go to the toilet. It was in an outhouse across the yard. I checked to make sure there was no one passing by, but the coast was clear so I quickly marched to the privy. It turned out to be a box over a hole in the ground. As I stood there I suddenly realised I was not alone. Around my feet waddled several ducks.

I returned to our room and found the farmer had delivered the daily newspaper. Blondie read me the news, as he was to do every morning whenever we were given the newspaper. Much of it was pure German propaganda, but the farmer, now and again, managed to hear the BBC on his radio and then passed on the news to us. We were greatly heartened when we heard that Monty and his Eighth Army had driven Rommel out of Agheila towards Tripoli.

We had thought to be there only a few days, but the days stretched into weeks. Finally Blondie asked the farmer why Marie-Claire had not come for us. Monsieur DuBois explained that he had not been able to contact her as he was not quite sure where she was. Asking us to be patient, he pointed out that we were quite safe where we were.

This was true. Thankfully, no Germans ever passed our way. Occasionally the farmer would come in and say there were gendarmes coming, and we would lie low in case they glanced through the window. Apart from those moments we were able to relax, but resting for too long was not good for us. We were used to being active and fit. Our legs grew stiff and weak for lack of exercise. We became impatient. It was worse for me than for Blondie. He always managed to keep himself occupied, either with his own thoughts or by reading. Among the books brought into us was a French translation of *Swiss Family Robinson* which he especially enjoyed.

It was frustrating for me, not being able to read the newspaper myself and having to rely on Blondie to translate everything. My thoughts often returned to England and going to the cinema or the pub. Blondie's thoughts were more to do with sailing, so we had little in common and small talk was at a minimum.

One day was like the next. Nothing to do. Nowhere to go, except for the occasional trip to the toilet where we often had to clear the snow off the box. Otherwise it was sit and read and eat and think. The novelty of the bed to sleep in, the regular meals and a roof over our heads had long gone.

Finally Blondie decided we should take up a hobby. 'Ever thought of woodcarving?' he asked me. 'Well, now's your chance.'

He asked Monsieur DuBois for a couple of penknives and we found some wood and set about carving it. Blondie had a real talent for it. He made a little goblin smoking a pipe. Meanwhile, I had become quite enchanted with the baby, a lovely little boy, about nine months old. I decided to make him some toys and started with an elephant. When I showed this to the parents they considered it a treasure. The boy still has it to this day.

We were confined to our room the whole of the time and saw very little of the family. Our meals were always brought into us; we mostly ate soup thick with beans. Sometimes we'd get a bit of lamb or chicken, supplied through underground contacts. But there was always plenty of red wine.

One day Madame DuBois entered with a plate of pancakes, followed by her husband, both of them beaming and saying something about 'Noël'.

I had not understood. Blondie looked at me and said softly, 'It's Christmas, Bill.'

I'd had no idea. I felt shattered. I unleashed my misery on the Major. 'But for this bloody mess we'd be at home with our families now. It's Christmas Day and here we are stuck in a French farmhouse, hoping to God we're going to get home all right. All for that soppy, bloody operation.'

He allowed me to go on and on, and when I had eventually finished complaining, he said, 'You feel better now?'

What a rotten bugger I was, I thought. This man had got to be feeling the same as me and he couldn't get back at me. Every time I exploded he just let me sound off. There must have been times when he felt as angry at me as I did at him, but he never showed it. In fact, despite my occasional outbursts I never really blamed him for my misfortunes. I had volunteered and gone willingly into the operation, and I have never regretted it. But there were times, such as that Christmas of 1942, when I just wished I was home with those I loved, enjoying turkey and Christmas pudding.

The DuBois family were not unsympathetic. They did their best to cheer us up and brought us a bottle of good red wine. And when I came to consider how some of our lads were spending Christmas in some ditch somewhere or in a POW camp, I realized that we were not badly off after all.

Then came the new year: 1943. I'll never forget the New Year's dinner they gave to us — roast duck. I thought, this is better than pancakes. Then I took one taste of it and, reeling from the strong sauce that covered it, said 'Gorblimey, this is bloody awful.'

'Don't you like it?' Blondie asked.

'Not one bit,' I said.

'Good, I can have yours.' And he did.

Another year had started unpromisingly and I wondered what else it had in store for us. We soon found out. One day Monsieur DuBois came into our room and told us he had bad news about Marie-Claire. She had met with an accident and was in hospital. As far as he could make out, a rival gang had tried to run her down with a lorry. She had nearly died, but was found by friends who saved her life.

We were naturally very sorry to hear of her misfortune, but none of this served to get us back to England. What would happen now, Blondie asked the farmer. He shrugged. Maybe another organization would come; he could not say. We must wait, we must be patient.

The Major must have braced himself for another of my outbursts at this news. But I bit my tongue. It was as much a blow to him as it was to me. Our hopes of escape and an end to the long waiting were dashed.

7

HE HAD HEARD FROM MARIE-CLAIRE: Monsieur DuBois's words gave us an immediate boost to the spirits. We had been hiding at the farm for close on a month and were growing ever more bored and frustrated. The farmer continued with the good news: her son would be coming to collect us in just a few days.

From that moment we waited anxiously for the arrival of this man who, we hoped, would lead us towards freedom. We were convinced we would soon be in Spain. The prospect of a long and difficult trek to the Spanish border looked appealing and undaunting.

A few days later Maurice, Marie-Claire's son, arrived. Nobody ever looked less like an agent. Nineteen years old, good-looking and speaking perfect English, he was more like an Oxford University student.

He was sorry that we'd been kept waiting for so long, he told us, but they had known nothing about us until Monsieur DuBois's message arrived a few weeks before. His mother would have immediately come to meet us herself but she was seriously hurt in an accident. But she was waiting for us in Lyons, which was where he would take us now.

Lyons was more than 200 miles from the Spanish border, Blondie remarked. 'Can we get through to Spain from there?'

'Yes, but not immediately. I'm afraid our usual route has been uncovered by the Gestapo, so we are trying to open another. In the meantime you will be safe in Lyons.'

So we were not going straight to the frontier; the thought was a blow. More hiding out somewhere in France, and for how long?

'Can you ride a bicycle?' Maurice asked. We both nodded. 'We are going to Roumazières by bicycle and from there we'll catch a train to Lyons. We'll start out after lunch.'

His manner in all this was a little too cavalier for my liking, as though this was all just some sort of schoolboy adventure. But otherwise he seemed to know exactly what he was about. He smiled and did his best to reassure us, but there was one problem.

'We can't get you any identity cards yet, not until we get to Lyons. So somehow I have to get you on the train without passing the barrier as there is usually a policeman inspecting everyone's identity cards.'

He would go into the station alone and buy our tickets. We should wait until the train was just leaving before getting on board, then we should find a seat at the end of a compartment. I would have to go straight to sleep, or at least pretend to sleep, so that no one would talk to me.

'If anyone does say anything,' Maurice said, 'just pretend you don't understand and sort of grunt "Breton". You'll pass easily enough for one of those peasants from Brittany who still don't speak French!'

We had our last lunch in that house alone in our room. I expressed my reservations to Blondie about travelling by train. To me it seemed that we would be sitting ducks. But that was the way these organizations operated, Blondie told me, working in the open and mingling with the crowds. It was the same as a criminal who finds it safer in a crowded town than in a quiet village where he stands out as a stranger. Besides, as Blondie pointed out, Maurice clearly had his wits about him, and I had to agree. He was as smart and shrewd as anyone I have ever met, and despite his manner I had complete confidence in him. He was a great lad.

Monsieur DuBois came into our room. 'Have you got anything English on you?' he asked.

Blondie translated for me and I told him I only had my identity discs. I kept them just in case we were captured, to prove we were British. Monsieur DuBois saw me fingering the discs and asked me to give them to him. Blondie told me to do as he wanted, so I handed them over.

Then there was the matter of our underclothes. Blondie told Monsieur DuBois that they were important to us because they had English labels. Monsieur DuBois demanded that we hand them over. Blondie refused. This might be our only way of proving we were British, he explained. It could be dangerous, the Frenchman warned. But Blondie told him we would take our chances.

Eventually Monsieur DuBois gave in. Wrapping up our change of underclothes in a parcel, he insisted that we keep it safe at all times. We should never let anyone else have the parcel or the consequences might be fatal.

The Major entrusted the parcel to me.

Now it was time to bid our farewells, and to thank the DuBois family who had taken such good care of us. But I was not sorry to say goodbye. I was excited and eager to move on. Outside we found only two bikes. I asked Maurice why.

'I can't ride,' he said cheerfully. 'One of you will have to give me a lift.'

'Just the job for you, Bill,' said Blondie.

With Maurice perched on my crossbar, we pedalled off down a track and came to a narrow road where we turned south. Maurice chatted merrily about his English mother and explained that it was a pro-German group that had tried to kill her. She had been left for dead, but fortunately one of her friends who was on the scene realized that she was still, if only barely, alive. Her friends quickly got her home and tended to her, and despite horrendous injuries she was recovering with remarkable speed. But then, as I was to discover, Mary Lindell was a remarkable woman.

It was growing dark when we finally arrived in Roumazières. We pulled up by a clump of bushes close to the railway junction. Telling us to wait here while he bought our tickets, Maurice explained that when we got to Lyons he would get off the train ahead of us and pass through the ticket barrier alone. He was known by the Gestapo there, so we could not be seen with him. And if he should get picked up we would have to make our way into town on our own.

'For now, keep watch,' he said. 'Stay out of sight.'

We stayed hidden behind the bushes and watched as Maurice went into the station. A short while later we saw him step onto the platform. A train pulled in and Maurice gave the signal that this was the one we wanted. It stood steaming and puffing as Maurice, among a crowd of people, climbed aboard. Biding our time, we waited for the right moment. With a loud hiss of steam and a whistle from the engine, the train began to pull slowly out of the station, passing us as it went. This was our cue. We sprang forward, sprinted across the tracks and leapt aboard.

We were on an open carriage. Although it was quite crowded, nobody batted an eyelid as we scrambled in. We made our way down to the end of the carriage. I found a seat, slumped down onto it and closed my eyes. I felt somebody brush my shoulder; it had to be Blondie taking his place next to me.

The train had gathered speed, rattling along and shaking us up.

My head dropped forward, bobbing about, as I gave an impression of a Frenchman asleep on a train. I was aware of my companion sitting next to me. But after a while I began to feel bothered; I just knew something was wrong. I slowly raised my head and opened my eyes to gaze into the mirror above the seat opposite me. There was Blondie all right, but he wasn't sitting next to me. He and Maurice were in the seats behind me and they were engaged in making small, cautious signals. They wanted me to get out of my seat. Why did they look so concerned, and who was my travelling companion?

Keeping every movement to a bare minimum, I glanced out of the corner of my eye and saw, sitting next to me, a German officer. My heart nearly stopped. He was glaring at me as if I had done something wrong. I knew that at any moment he would say something. I tried not to look alarmed although my pulse was racing and beads of perspiration formed above my eyes. He continued to glare at me, and I imagined that he was flipping through a mental chart of suspected agents.

I didn't hesitate a moment longer. I shot out of my seat to join Maurice and the Major. Then it struck me that I might have made a fatal mistake. In evacuating that seat so fast I might have given the German officer cause to take umbrage. Or I might have aroused further suspicions. I just knew he would get up and come over to ask why I had left in such a hurry. I watched his back, waiting to see him move. The seconds passed, turning into minutes, and still he remained in his seat. The danger had passed and I began to breathe easily again.

I tried to sleep that night as we were bounced about in our seats. Occasionally I dropped off, only to be woken by the train screeching to a halt at a station. Often the train shunted to and fro. Passengers came and went. It was impossible to sleep restfully. I thought the night would never end.

Eventually it did. The next morning, as we pulled into Lyons, Maurice rose and headed for the door. We followed a short way behind, mingling with the crowd that jostled towards the barrier where gendarmes and German troops stood guard. Ahead of us, Maurice handed in his ticket and passed through the barrier. The Major went next. He encountered no problem.

With the parcel of underclothes tucked under my arm, I reached the barrier and handed in my ticket. A gendarme looked me over. I pretended not to notice him, but before I could hurry through, he spoke to me. I froze and looked blankly at him. He spoke again, sounding agitated. All I could respond with was a vague expression. He spoke again and pointed at the parcel under my arm. He was trying to get hold of it, and by now he was getting annoyed that I had not replied. Clearly he wanted to know what was in the parcel. But I could give no answer. A further moment's hesitation and he would arrest me and call for the troops. He was trying to yank the parcel away, and I suddenly decided to let him have it. I just let go of it as he grabbed it, and hurried on with the rest of the crowd.

I had no idea how long it would take him to unwrap the parcel and discover its contents, or even if he would notice the English labels, but I wasn't waiting around to find out. He might have ordered me to wait but I did not understand. Streaming with perspiration, I hurried with the crowd into the street. At any moment I expected to feel a heavy hand on my shoulder. If I was stopped now, I didn't have a hope in hell of bluffing my way out of it.

The Major was waiting for me. I caught up with him and said, 'Some bloody gendarme's got my parcel.'

'Oh hell! We'd better keep up with Maurice. Don't look back. Just keep walking.'

We hurried on down the street, knowing that by now the gendarme must have opened the parcel. Maurice was waiting at the end of the street, but he didn't allow us to catch up with him; he was obviously intent on keeping a discreet distance between himself and us. He stepped onto a tram and we hurried after him, expecting a troop of soldiers to come after us at any moment. Maurice was just paying his fare as we stepped on board. We watched how much he paid and then Blondie bought tickets for himself and me. People poured onto the car. It seemed as though the tram would never go. I kept looking back to see if there were any soldiers in pursuit. Finally, the tram moved off and the street and the station at the top of it passed out of view.

The car was packed full and I was jostled along, separated from Blondie and Maurice. I prayed that nobody would speak to me. We rumbled on through the streets of Lyons. I was alarmed to see, through the windows, so many German soldiers out on the streets. It seemed inconceivable to me that we could pass unnoticed through a town swarming with Jerries. So far Lady Luck had smiled down on us but I felt certain that she would abandon us at any moment.

The tram came to a halt and Maurice got off, followed by the Major. I pushed my way through the car and got out, hurrying after them. Blondie waited for me to catch up with him while Maurice strode on ahead. We finally came to a block of flats and, once inside, Maurice turned and said, 'Well done.' He really seemed to be enjoying the whole experience.

We climbed the stairs. This was no dowdy, run-down tenement but a block of luxury apartments. Maurice knocked at a door. It opened and we followed Maurice inside. Entering the front room we found a small, middle-aged woman in a Red Cross uniform. Her leg was in plaster and she had heavy strapping around her collar bone.

'This,' said Maurice, 'is my mother.'

'I am so sorry that you had to hide out for so long at the farm,' Mary Lindell said. 'I'm afraid my route across the Pyrenees has closed and I've got to open a new way through. Now, come and have some lunch.'

There was something of the English matron about her. She was fearless, a touch arrogant, but very jovial. And although she was a woman, she was very much the governor. I had arrived feeling unsure about putting my life in the hands of a woman, but within ten minutes I had every confidence in her.

We sat down to a very convivial lunch with Mary as well as the elderly and obviously wealthy couple who owned the flat. They were Jewish, which was surprising in the middle of a German-occupied town. I had the impression that the man was someone of position, probably someone that the Germans needed, and for that reason they never took him and his wife away. And yet he could not have been a collaborator as such or Mary would have had them shot without a moment's hesitation.

When lunch was over she began questioning us, something we had grown quite used to, and by now we realized that this kind of interrogation was essential because often escaping RAF men turned out to be German agents.

'Where were you born?' she asked me.

'In the East End of London.'

'I know it well,' she said, and then she got me to talk about that part of London. Whether she really knew anything about the East End I don't know for sure, but she made me believe she did.

'So you are the Commanding Officer of the unit,' she said to

Blondie. 'And no doubt you have been gathering information on the way.'

Blondie agreed that we had picked up quite a bit of information. In fact, we had written down in code everything we had seen that we thought might be valuable; troop movements, anti-aircraft positions, the German occupation of St Même-les-Carrières and so on.

Finally satisfied that we were the genuine articles, she said, 'Well, Major, I shall be sending you home in about three nights by plane.'

'That's wonderful news,' said Blondie. 'But what about Bill?'

'He'll have to wait, I'm afraid. There's only room for one passenger.'

'Can't you ask them to send another plane for me?' I said.

'I'm afraid they'll only do that for an officer, not for a private. At least you, Major, will be home and safe within a few days.'

'Forget it,' Blondie suddenly said. 'If Bill can't go, neither shall I. We started this off together, and we're going through it together — all the way.'

I couldn't believe my ears. My respect and admiration for him grew tenfold that day. Then I decided to ask Mary a few things that had bugged me for weeks. 'Tell me,' I said. 'Why is it we've found the French people so hostile? We would knock at a farmhouse and have the door slammed in our face. Even those Maquis fellows gave us a hard time. I thought they were supposed to be our friends.'

'I can't understand it happening in that area of the country,' she said. 'Do you speak French?'

'No.'

'What about you?' she said to Blondie.

'Yes, I do,' he replied.

'Speak to me in French.' Blondie spoke a few words. Mary threw up her hands and said. 'Oh my God, no wonder! You speak French with a German accent.'

Blondie had learnt to speak French while at Oxford, and his teacher had tried so hard to get him to speak French without an Oxford accent that Blondie had ended up with a German accent instead. No wonder every Frenchman he spoke to thought he was a German agent.

During the First World War Mary Lindell had worked for the Red Cross. After the war she had married a French count, effectively becoming the Comtesse de Milleville. When the Second World War broke out the count refused to fight, so Mary kicked him out. Now she was fighting the Germans her own way. She was still an officer in the Red Cross, but she was also the leader of an escape organization.

Mary lived high up in an apartment block with her young daughter, Barbie. Like her mother, Barbie hated the Germans. One day she was standing on the veranda and, looking down, she saw a high-ranking German officer with his French lady who wore a large rimmed hat. Barbie leaned forward and spat.

Plop! It landed on the woman's hat. She and the officer looked up to see who had dared to insult them in this way and just caught sight of the girl disappearing inside. The German was furious and flew up the stairs. He banged on the door of Mary's flat.

'What's all the panic?' Mary asked calmly.

'Somebody has just insulted my good lady,' he ranted.

'Well, what have you come here for?'

'Because it was someone in this flat.'

'There is no one here except my daughter and myself,' she said.

The officer looked past Mary and saw Barbie. 'That's her,' he cried.

'But she's just a child. What did she do?'

'She spat on the lady's hat.'

'Really?' said Mary incredulously. 'What a good shot.'

Her attitude left the German speechless. There was nothing he could do to gain satisfaction from a child, and so he stormed off, tramping down the stairs. Mary had no fear of the Germans; not even when they arrested her on a charge of being a British agent.

'You're a defeated nation,' a German general told her.

'Not at all,' she said. 'You'll never defeat Great Britain, I'm afraid.'

'We shall see,' said the general. 'As for you, I'm putting you in prison for the next nine months.'

'Nine months?' she said. 'Marvellous! Just time for me and Adolf to have a baby!'

She was then locked away but refused to clean her cell out. The prison's commanding officer came to her cell and told her, 'You *must* clean out your cell.'

She told him, 'I must certainly *not*. I'm not a char woman.'

'You *will* clean the cell out.'

Mary remained immovable. 'I'm British and no one tells me what to do. Especially not you.'

'If you do not clean your cell out,' ranted the officer, 'I will have you executed for disobeying my orders.'

'Carry on then,' she said, unendingly defiant.

The next day two guards came to her cell, escorted her out into the courtyard and placed her up against a wall. Opposite her stood the firing squad.

The officer slowly paced up to her and said, 'Now are you going to clean your cell out?'

She looked him in the eye and said, 'Certainly not.'

The officer flew into a blind rage, but there was nothing he could do to frighten this arrogant British woman into submission. He ordered the firing squad to stand down and had Mary returned to her cell.

She survived her nine months imprisonment and was released to continue her activities in the Red Cross and the French underground.

'That moustache is going to come off,' Mary told Blondie. He was dismayed and tried to argue with her. In vain. 'You can't go around Lyons sporting a moustache like that,' she told him. 'You look too English.'

The Major had often remarked to me that no one would ever make him remove his flowing, golden moustache. Now here he was, being ordered to shave it off by a Red Cross officer, and a woman at that. He finally agreed to trim it down and went off to the bathroom. He returned with just a tiny bit trimmed off.

Mary inspected the moustache. 'It's still too much,' she said. 'Back to the bathroom.'

He reluctantly went back to trim a bit more off, but she was still not satisfied and sent him back again. He finally ended up with a neat, small moustache that was to her satisfaction.

'Now, you cannot stay here,' said Mary, 'but we have got somewhere else for you to stay. I don't know the owners of this place, but Maurice does. We shall have some photographs taken of you to go in the identity papers we will get for you. Incidentally, I have a very strict rule. You are not to involve yourself with any women.'

I was wondering what the harm was in a little flirtation with a French lass, but before I had a chance to ask, Maurice led us out into the street and onto another tram. He was taking us to the photographers. Mary had a contact at the town hall who was able to supply perfectly authentic identity cards. We became real people who had either disappeared or died.

I asked Maurice how the French felt about the English.

'Some like you, some don't,' he said. 'It's an even split, about fifty-fifty, I would say.'

'What about the young — the young *women*, for instance?'

He smiled. 'If the girls knew there were Englishmen here they'd storm the house.'

'Do me a favour, Maurice.'

'What's that?' he asked.

'Tell 'em where we're living.'

'Oh no, no! You heard my mother. No women!'

After we'd had our photographs taken Maurice took us to another flat in another block, occupied by a woman. We entered her home, thankful that we would have no more running to do for a while. We were shown to a very nicely furnished room. This was more like it, Blondie remarked, and I agreed it was very nice and comfortable.

The woman seemed alarmed to hear us speaking English. She called Maurice to one side and muttered angrily to him. It turned out that she did not want any Englishmen in her home. Maurice tried to reason with her but she grew even more furious. She ended by announcing that she would report our presence to the police. And she pushed past him and left the flat.

Maurice hustled us out, explaining that he had misjudged this woman, that she was a German sympathizer and was already on her way to fetch the gendarmes.

We returned to where Mary was staying with the old Jewish couple. She was furious when she heard what had happened. 'That woman is a traitor,' she said. 'Well, we'll just have to send her a little parcel.'

The next morning a parcel was put through the woman's letterbox. Not long after, there was an explosion in her flat. That's how life was in France during the war. Mary could not risk having anyone reveal her organization.

She told us how she was once faced with a Canadian who was so terrified that he kept crying and clinging on to her. She told him to pull himself together, but still he sobbed and clung to her. 'You're a danger to yourself and to everyone else, including me,' she told him.

Then she drew a revolver, pointed it at his head, and said, 'If you don't pull yourself together I'm going to shoot you.' He quickly stopped crying.

Blondie asked her, 'Would you really have shot him?'

'Oh yes,' she replied. 'He could have put all the people escaping, as well as us, at risk if he'd carried on like that.' She could not afford to be sentimental when the security of her organization was at stake.

One day Mary came to us and asked for our advice. 'I've had a chap come through; he was shot down in a Spitfire but I'm very suspicious about him. He reckons he's a Group Captain.',

That was very, very unlikely, we told her. You didn't usually get Group Captains flying Spitfires in hostile territory.

'This is what worried me,' said Mary. 'Thanks for your help.'

What happened to this man, or whether he was a Group Captain or not, we never knew. He certainly never came through the escape route while we were about. But she had to be ruthless; she had encountered Germans who spoke perfect English, some having been educated in England, and they knew all the right answers to her careful questions.

Later Blondie and I spoke about this. If he really had been a Group Captain, Blondie remarked, and if Mary had done away with him on our say so . . . It didn't bear thinking about.

'But all we did was tell her what we thought,' I said. 'What more could we do?'

If he was a German, and she hadn't caught on to him, the whole escape organization would have been exposed and we would have been captured. These were decisions Mary had to make all the time. We did not envy her.

Mary had found another safe house for us, and again Maurice was to lead the way. But before we left Blondie wrote a coded message for Mary to send to Britain, informing COHQ what had taken place and that we were still alive.

About a month had passed since Mackinnon and Conway had said farewell to Monsieur and Madame Jaubert. So it was with great joy that news finally reached Monsieur Jaubert concerning the two Englishmen he and his wife had grown so fond of. But joy soon turned to heartbreak as the Jauberts learned that, having successfully reached La Réole, they had been taken prisoner.

111

Anxious for further news, Monsieur Jaubert wrote to the mayor of La Réole who responded with all the news he possessed regarding Mackinnon and Conway.

In La Réole the Marines had been admitted to a civilian hospital and for a short while it seemed they were safe. But someone betrayed them. Towards the end of December, a squad of Germans had swooped on the hospital and arrested the Englishmen. The mayor had no further news, and it would not be for months to come that Monsieur and Madame Jaubert would learn of what befell Mackinnon and Conway.

Meanwhile, back in England, there was concern at COHQ. A month or so earlier they had picked up the German radio announcement which had claimed that on 8 December 'a small British sabotage squad was engaged at the mouth of the Gironde River and finished off in combat'.

But in a letter to the Prime Minister, Lord Mountbatten wrote that it seemed possible that the Germans had only intercepted one section of the raiding party.

It was decided to get some aerial photographs of the harbour at Bordeaux, and from these photographs Combined Ops were able to assess much of the damage, confirming that, at the very least, some of the party had made it that far.

Now Mountbatten became anxious to know if there had been news of any survivors from the Frankton operation. There was no news, he was told. He remarked that he had been persuaded against his better judgement to let Major Hasler go on the raid: 'Now we have lost him.'

On 25 January we were all reported 'Missing, presumed dead', and the appropriate 'We regret to inform you' telegrams were sent to all the families concerned.

After Blondie had given his coded message to Mary to send, we set off through the streets of Lyons with Maurice just ahead of us. Passing German soldiers, I still found it unnerving to be walking so openly before the eyes of the enemy.

We boarded another crowded tram which took us to the outskirts of town. Then Maurice led us to one of a row of large houses. Here we met a woman and her daughter. The woman's husband was also in the house, Maurice said, but we would not see him. 'He's a German sympathizer. But don't worry, he's bedridden. Fortunately for us, two weeks ago he was run down by a tram and lost both his legs.'

Couldn't have happened to a nicer fellow, I thought.

His wife and daughter were on our side, however, and they would take care of us, Maurice added and then he left.

The mother and daughter thereafter called us by our first names, but we never learned theirs; we were discouraged from trying to learn anyone's names because of the danger to them if we were captured. But they took great care of us, making our stay pleasant, supplying us with good food. We didn't see too much of them, confined to our room as we were, but the girl occasionally came in to see us as she was learning to speak English.

One day the mother came in looking flushed and fearful. The Germans were conducting a house-to-house search, she told us. We would have to hide in the garden.

We hurried out of our room, keeping as quiet as we could; the bedridden man must not hear us. If he learned now that we were in his house, he might well tell the Germans. We rushed out into the large garden and hid among the shrubs, hardly daring to breathe.

Soldiers were sweeping through one house after the next, searching every room, looking in every cupboard and searching every garden. We kept our heads, listening to the Germans stomping about in next-door's garden. They finished that search and we knew they would be coming into our house any moment. We quickly scrambled over the fence into the next garden and hid low while the soldiers tramped through the house. We waited, wondering if the husband had indeed informed the Germans that he had heard intruders in his house. Several minutes passed. We had been careful to ensure there was nothing in our room to betray our presence. We heard them come into the garden, the officer barking orders as they continued their search. Then they left.

We climbed back over the fence and returned to our room. This was nothing new, our hostess told us. The soldiers had been before and they would probably come again. And they did. And each time we did the same as before, hiding in the garden and jumping across into next-door's garden at the right moment. The bedridden man never knew we were there.

One evening Mary came to visit us in person; we guessed that this meant she had bad news. We were right. Once again her escape route had been betrayed. She had no alternative but to find another way through to Spain.

'How long will that take?' Blondie asked.

'It could be weeks. So I think the best thing is to hand you over to another organization.'

My heart sank into my boots. I had come to trust Mary without reservation and felt that she was our best hope of escape.

'I am sorry,' she said, 'but you don't want to hang about here, do you? I'm sure you'd much rather be going as soon as possible, wouldn't you? Very well, then. Come with me. I shall take you to someone else who can help you.'

Once more we boarded a tram and once more it was crowded. I was jostled away up the car leaving Blondie and Mary at the other end. I kept my eyes on them to make sure I didn't miss the getting off point. But when we reached our destination she called out in English, 'I say, Bill, we're getting off here.'

Everybody turned to look at me. I tried to shrink down inside my shirt collar and slid out through the door.

I found Mary doubled up with laughter. I was damp with perspiration from her little prank. Why she did it I'll never know, but she had enjoyed giving me one last scare.

We wandered through the streets as the dusk settled over Lyons. Mary stopped. Ahead of us a man lurked in the shadows. Seeing us, he stepped out of the shadows and walked towards us, looking cautiously about. He took Mary's hand and shook it, then shook our hands. His name was Carter, he told us, and he was English.

'Well,' Mary said to us, 'Mr Carter will take good care of you.'

I still felt that Mary was our best hope of escape. Somehow, this Mr Carter didn't seem to match up to Mary, based on my first impression of him. With Mary, you knew immediately that she knew what she was doing and you had complete faith in her. Mr Carter failed to instil such confidence in me.

It turned out that this organization was actually larger than Mary's. It was run by a French-Canadian who did it for money; Mary did it for patriotism. Mary saw us all as individuals and she cared for each individual. To this other organization we were just a type of merchandise. As all this came through to me, I felt disheartened and depressed. Nevertheless, we had to rely on somebody and Mary seemed to trust these people.

'Good luck to you both,' she said. 'Cheer up, Bill, you'll soon be on your way home.'

I thanked her as warmly as I knew how. Mary wasn't only a courageous and highly organized underground fighter, but a good friend too. I was going to miss her and my heart was heavy. I couldn't help but wonder if, with her incredible devil-may-care bravado, she would be able to evade the Germans for much longer.

Mary Lindell was in the process of taking an Englishman to Spain by train. As they pulled into their station she looked out of the window. Standing on the platform were Gestapo officers. She knew they were waiting for her.

'You'll have to get out the other side,' she told the escapee. Her plan was to allow herself to be caught as a diversion for the Englishman to get away. She stepped down off the train, knowing that she was walking into a trap. The Gestapo officers immediately descended on her and led her away. She had been betrayed by one of her own people.

She underwent interrogation at the hands of the Gestapo but she told them nothing. When they finally had enough of her, they decided to send her to Auschwitz. Handcuffed and guarded by a Gestapo officer, she was put on a train.

She told her guard she had to go to the toilet and persuaded him to remove her handcuffs. However, he followed her along the carriage to the toilet. She went inside and locked the door. The officer stood by the window, watching to see if she should try to jump. He had his gun ready, just in case.

The train was travelling at speed, but Mary opened the window and jumped. The German's gun fired three times and she thumped heavily on to the ground, rolling over and over. She had caught one bullet in her cheek, one in her head and another in her shoulder.

The German pulled the emergency cord and the train screeched to a halt. He jumped from the carriage and ran back to where Mary lay, seemingly lifeless. But to his astonishment, she was alive, although unconscious. She had somehow cheated death again.

He put her broken body back on the train and she was taken on to Auschwitz. There she was operated on by a surgeon who knew of her; she had become quite famous for her exploits. The doctor battled to save her, operating on her for hours, and won.

When she was fully recovered, the doctor asked her to work alongside him; she had valuable medical knowledge and, besides, the doctor had a warm regard for her. So in that place which for thousands was hell on earth, Mary worked with the doctor, doing whatever she could to relieve the suffering of so many.

When the day of liberation finally approached, and with just twenty-four hours before the Allies arrived, the Germans decided that the prisoners who knew too much had to be killed. This meant executing at least half the camp, Mary among them.

When the doctor heard the news, he went straight to Mary. 'Your name is going to be called out tomorrow,' he told her. 'Don't go. You and half the camp are to be slaughtered. Try to get yourself among those who are to be spared.'

The next day the prisoners were paraded. Names were called. Prisoners and other non-German prison personnel stepped forward, unaware of the fate that awaited them. Then came Mary's name. She carefully began to move, as if going to join the others, but she managed to slip back among those who were to live. When all the names had been read off, the poor unfortunate souls were led away and shot — just hours before the Germans ran away and the Allies arrived.

Bewildered prisoners, barely more than walking skeletons, stared through lifeless eyes as Allied jeeps drove into the camp. The soldiers were soon to learn of the horrors that had taken place there. Mary Lindell, who had been marked for execution for knowing too much, wasted no time in telling the Allies exactly what had been going on and who had been responsible.

For a woman who had been so active in the French underground movement, who had shown such open hostility to the Germans, who had been run down, imprisoned, interrogated, shot, imprisoned and included on a death list, Mary Lindell was a miracle. She survived the war, as did hundreds of British men because of her. To say that she was wonderful is a total understatement.

8

'WELL, BILL, WE'LL GET YOU TO your house of safety,'
Carter said, 'and then we'll take Major Hasler on to his.'

'What?' I blurted in astonishment. 'You mean, you're separating
us?'

It was only for a short while, he replied, but he was not winning
me over.

'Bloody good start this is,' I moaned to myself.

We followed him through the back streets and finally came to a
narrow alley. We turned into it and halfway down entered a small
house. This was my hide-out, Carter told me.

Inside, an elderly couple greeted me with smiles which did nothing
to quell my dark mood. The woman looked me up and down and
said, in English, 'You are just a boy, too young to be a soldier,'

I was twenty years old. I felt like fifty. I was shown to my room
and Carter said that on no condition should I leave it.

The couple had a daughter in her mid twenties, a hard-looking,
very masculine girl. I couldn't help seeing the amorous looks she kept
giving me. The Major had noticed; he grinned and said, 'I think
you're going to be all right here, Bill.'

I didn't like this situation at all. If she were to make any advances
towards me and I rejected her, which was the only likely scenario, a
whole can of worms might get opened up. She might even turn me
over to the gendarmes. I hoped it would not come to this. Of course,
the easy solution might have been to give in to her, but for one thing
I found her not in the least bit attractive, and furthermore I did not
want to risk the outrage of her parents.

Then Blondie and Carter left, with Carter assuring me I would
only be there for a few days.

I had thought to be confined to my room the whole time, as Carter
had said, but in fact the couple did their best to make me feel at home,
inviting me into the front room. Monsieur asked me if I played
draughts and I told him I was born playing draughts.

This was going to be easy, I thought as he began setting up the board. After we'd made a couple of moves, he took his piece and, with a triumphant laugh, jumped over all my pieces and swept the board.

'You can't do that,' I protested.

'Ah, but these are French rules,' he said.

'French rules? I was playing by British rules.'

'Then I shall teach you how to play the French way,' he said, and no matter how much I protested, he insisted that I be his pupil. Consequently, during my whole stay I never won a game. I'm sure the bandit was making up his 'French rules' as we went along, making the most unconventional moves I have ever seen on a draughts board. I thought he was a cheating old swine. But it kept him happy.

During the day their daughter was at work, I was relieved to discover; but when she came home, the first thing she did was come to my room. She sat down, chatting away and openly flirting. I kept one eye on her, the other on the door. I remembered what Maurice had said: 'If the young girls knew where you lived, they'd storm the house.' If this one started storming, I thought, I would start retreating.

I was relieved when a young Frenchwoman arrived one morning to take me away. There was no warning that anyone might come for me, and when she arrived I had no idea who she was. But the couple obviously knew her well enough and I guessed that she was a member of the organization. She spoke to me in broken English, explaining that she would take me to Major Hasler.

This was heartening news; I suddenly realized how much I had missed Blondie during the days apart.

I said goodbye to my host family and followed my new guide. After a short walk we came across Carter and the Major waiting for us; I was delighted to see Blondie again. The four of us boarded a tram which was typically crowded, but by now I had come to realize this was the safest form of travel because I never saw a German travelling on trams. The soldiers were warned by their officers to stay away from crowds because too many Germans had been found strangled to death in dark alleys, or with their throats cut, or even beheaded. A solitary German in a tram crowded with Frenchmen could easily wind up the same way.

Such discoveries enraged the Germans and had them dashing round the streets in cars and armoured vans, swooping on houses. Very patriotic of the French, but it wasn't good for us at all. I always thought it would be a nasty twist if we should end up being taken away and shot as a reprisal.

The tram took us to the edge of town. After a lengthy walk we came to a large empty house, standing in spacious grounds. The first thing I noticed as we entered was the huge marble stairway curving graciously up to the upper floor. It was very grand.

'You'll be safe here for a while,' Carter said. Nobody was likely to come here. We could do as we liked. He pointed out the various exits available to us if somebody should come sneaking around, and then, ensuring we were left with a good supply of food, he left with the Frenchwoman.

It was all very well being left on our own, but the thought struck me that this organization was very unlike Mary's; she would keep watch over us like a mother hen, or at least have someone trustworthy to look out for our welfare. Here, alone in this secluded house, if anything went wrong we were on our own. We could expect no help from Mr Carter's people.

We explored the house at our leisure. On the upper floor we found a piano. 'Excellent,' Blondie explained, and he gave me his rendering of 'Be Like the Kettle and Sing'.

'That's not bad,' I said. 'Not very good, but not bad.' He played it again and I asked what else he could play.

'Nothing else,' he said, 'only this,' and he played 'Be Like the Kettle and Sing' again. 'I need more practice.'

He could say that again, I thought. Then he asked me to help him move the piano downstairs. He didn't want to have to come all the way up here every time he wanted to play.

We slowly eased the piano to the top of the marble stairway, 'Steady, steady,' he said as we brought it to the top step. 'So far so good. Let's ease your side of it down onto the next step.'

Straining to keep it from running away by itself, we attempted to lower it to the next step. I knew we'd never do it. I could feel the piano slipping from my grasp. I couldn't hold on. Then it was off. It bumped down to the next step of its own accord, then the next step and then the next, gathering speed as it went. We could do nothing to hold it back, and took off after it as it went bumping and sliding all the way to the bottom and beating us by yards in the race to the ground floor.

'Well, that's one way to shift a piano,' I said.

Blondie ran his fingers across the keys. Something close to 'Be Like the Kettle and Sing' emanated from it, only slightly more out of tune than before. 'Just need a little more practice,' he said with glee, and played it again. By now I was getting sick and tired of 'Be Like the Kettle and Sing', and I sauntered off to explore on my own.

In one of the rooms I came across a musical box. I turned the handle which set a cardboard disc with holes revolving, which in turn activated little wires that pinged out a tune, 'Orpheus in the Underworld'.

'Look what I found,' I said to Blondie, and gave him a rendition of 'Orpheus in the Underworld'. I could speed up the tune or slow it down depending on how fast I turned the handle. He was unimpressed. He played another encore of 'Be Like the Kettle and Sing'. So I turned the handle again. He played louder. I played faster. Over and over, louder and louder, faster and faster until we were both too hysterical to continue.

'I'll tell you what,' Blondie said at last, controlling his laughter. 'If you promise not to play that awful tune, I'll stop playing the piano.'

Days passed. Boredom, a fierce enemy, set in. We returned to woodcarving to keep us occupied. At least we had room to move about in and keep active, if only on a limited scale. It was a relief when Carter finally returned. It was early February.

It was time for us to move on, Carter announced. He would take us to the station to meet two couriers who would accompany us to Marseilles.

More guides, another French town; when would we finally cross into Spain? It was difficult for us to appreciate the complications involved in the whole process, but although it seemed to us that we were just being shifted from pillar to post, we were in fact gradually, if painfully slowly, moving up the line in an escape programme. Dressed in one of the suits Maurice had given me, I looked like quite a respectable Frenchman now.

One last tram journey through Lyons took us to the station that evening and there we met our couriers, two men. We thanked Carter and the French lady and followed the two men onto the train, finding a third-class compartment which was, as usual, quite crowded. With a shrill whistle, the engine chugged into action.

One of our new guides decided to entertain his fellow Frenchmen with a succession of funny stories that had them all in fits of laughter. This, I thought, put me at risk, and Blondie too, in fact. They might expect us to join in the conversation. Then where would we be with me not being able to speak a word and Blondie speaking French with a German accent?

But in fact our jovial companion was speaking to everyone to prevent them from speaking to us. The French are by nature sociable people, ready to talk to strangers. The more he talked, the more they laughed, and while he remained the centre of attention nobody bothered to speak to me or Blondie at all.

We rattled on through the night. Into the carriage came a gendarme.

'He wants to see identity cards,' Blondie whispered to me.

The gendarme stood above me and I held my breath as he took my card and glanced over it. This was the moment of truth. I prayed that Mary had had a good job done on the card, and that the gendarme would not ask me any questions. He passed the card back to me and went on to check Blondie's. He seemed to be in some hurry in checking everyone's identity cards; maybe he was tired and wanted to go back to sleep. He carried on down the carriage. The danger had passed.

Morning came and we pulled into Marseilles. I wondered how close we were to making the crossing over into Spain. Or would we be staying at another safehouse for more intolerable weeks? We climbed out of the train and moved swiftly towards the barrier. Standing there was a German soldier, checking all identity cards. God, don't let him speak to me, I prayed as I handed him my card. He looked it over, checking my face against the photograph. I remained as impassive as I could, desperate not to betray myself with any sign of fear. He handed back the card and I hurried on. Blondie came through easily as well.

Our escorts led us to a high block of flats and we caught the elevator to the top floor. On the way up I remarked that if there were a raid on this place we would have no chance of escape.

'Not so,' said one of the escorts who spoke a little English. 'There is an escape route over the roof.'

But at eight storeys up we hoped we would not have to use it.

We arrived at the top floor, stepped out of the elevator and approached a door. One of the escorts knocked and the door was opened by a slim, dark woman. We were introduced; her name was Madame Martin. Inside we met her two little daughters, one aged about eleven and the other seven. Her husband worked at the docks; we would meet him that evening when he came home.

'It will not be long now,' said one of the guides; we were grateful for that.

Monsieur and Madame Martin were lovely people, doing all they could to make us comfortable. He was something of a roughneck and a Communist whose brother was a champion boxer; after the war, his brother fought our champion, Bruce Woodcock (and lost).

Their younger girl took a shine to me. She also knew how to take the mickey and decided to try and teach me French, mainly because she thought my pathetic attempts at French were hilarious. She would carefully shape her mouth to show me how to pronounce a word, getting me to copy her. But each time she'd roll up with laughter as I came out with the wrong sounds, and that set the others off laughing too, which delighted her even more. I knew she was sending me up but she was adorable.

The girls must have been experienced in the task of assisting escapees for they never spoke a word at school about it; to do so would have been our undoing, as well as their parents'. Over the weeks, others joined us on the escape line.

One of these later arrivals was Werner de Merode, a Belgian prince and a Spitfire pilot who spoke perfect English, having been educated in England. He smoked cigarettes through a very long holder; a real school-tie merchant, I thought. He annoyed me because, although much of the time we were without cigarettes, he always had a supply for himself. In fact, I didn't like him at all. He was arrogant and smarmy. I often felt like giving him a thump.

We were also joined by Edit. She weighed at least sixteen stone. Considering the harrowing experience she had survived, she was extremely jolly and spoke very good English for a Frenchwoman.

Edit had been working with a British radio operator when they were both captured by the Gestapo and taken away to be interrogated. Upon arriving at Gestapo headquarters, the Britisher made a dive for the window, plunging to the street below. Edit had no idea if he had survived the fall or not, but when all the Germans raced out of the room and into the street to get him, she quickly followed them and, once outside, slipped away. She now hoped to escape to Britain to join up with the Free French.

Two other would-be escapers were RAF boys who had bailed out of their bomber when hit during a raid. It became quite crowded in the flat, but there were plenty of beds or mattresses for us all to sleep on, and despite our numbers no one went hungry. Sometimes friends arrived with a whole dead sheep which they dumped in the bath and cut up. For several days after, we fed on lamb. Each day Madame Martin went out early and bought food on the black market. Much of what she cooked was soaked in garlic which wasn't much to my liking, but there were lots of vegetables to fill me up.

We passed much of the time playing cards, but despite all the companionship and the generous supply of food, we grew ever more restless. I would sit by the window and gaze out at Marseilles. Somehow it reminded me of home. From up there on the eighth floor it was not difficult to imagine I was back in London. I wanted to get out of the flat, go down there and be among it all. I was more homesick than ever, and frustrated at not being able to do anything about it. It was wait, wait, wait.

As the long days passed I found Edit to be particularly companionable. She too tried to teach me French, again with hilarious results. I mispronounced words, and she twisted my mispronunciation to sound like something rude which had the others in stitches. Even Blondie came in for his share of mocking.

After one meal, she asked Blondie in French if he wanted any more to eat. He replied, also in French, 'No, I'm full,' which apparently meant something very rude to the French and had Edit and the Martins rolling on the floor. Blondie and I hadn't a clue what it meant, but just sat there feeling utterly daft.

'What did I say?' Blondie asked me.

'Search me,' I said. 'I don't think I'll ever conquer the language.' And I was right. I never did.

Edit and I had become close friends, but she was beginning to show that she wanted to get even closer. Here we go again, I thought as she began making eyes at me.

I was delighted when Jack Dawson, one of the RAF lads, told me that he fancied Edit. 'You think I stand any chance with her?' he asked.

'I don't see why not, Jack. Give it your best shot, mate.' I hoped he would succeed and take the pressure off me. But she didn't want to know Jack. It was me she wanted. She was a lovely person, a good friend, but not someone I wanted to be intimate with. At least she was not going to turn me over to the gendarmes if I rejected her. Although it did occur to me that she was so big she might have thrown me through the window. Fortunately, there was no privacy in the flat and so she never had the chance to make any real attempt to seduce me.

After a month in the flat we were all going slightly insane, desperate for the day to come when we would cross the Pyrenees into Spain. And that in itself was becoming a problem for we had been unable to get any kind of exercise. We were growing fat and soft. The trek across the Pyrenees would be hard, and I began to wonder how well the Major and I – since we had actually been in hiding far longer than the others – would fare in our softened condition, trying to climb those snow-covered mountains.

There was much activity and excitement in an Intelligence office back in London. It was 23 February and a coded message had been received from 'Marie-Claire'. But the code seemed unfamiliar to the decoding section; all they could be sure of was that it had been sent by Major Hasler.

During our training we had all been taught how to use Code No.3, but by the time Blondie came to write his message for Mary Lindell to send he had forgotten exactly how to use it. He asked me but I had forgotten too. He just did the best he could and hoped that somebody would be able to decipher it.

That somebody turned out to be a Wren officer, Marie Hamilton. She worked throughout the night on it, assuming that the Major had tried to use Code No.3, and by morning she was beginning to crack it. Before long she had the whole of the decoded message on its way to Combined Ops HQ.

Blondie had told the story from when we launched our five cockles from the *Tuna*, explaining how one of the canoes was damaged and how the other three cockles were lost before we made it to Bordeaux where we completed our mission. As one of the Combined Ops officers read through the message, he paused for a moment, puzzled by what the message said following the report of the raid.

'What does this mean? *Back to get her same night?*'

This completely foxed the men of British Intelligence, until somebody realized that there had been one mistake in the decoding. It was meant to read, *'Back together same night,'* and went on, *'Separate and scuttle cockles one mile north of Blaye. Sparks with me. Fate of Crayfish crew unknown. Hasler.'*

It was the last day of February 1943 when the French-Canadian who ran this escape organization turned up at the apartment. He was heavily built with ginger hair and spoke only French. His name was Pat — we were not to learn his surname, nor even if Pat was his real name. To me he looked like a real villain. Perhaps I should have felt grateful to the man, but he was pocketing a lot of money from the British Government for saving our lives. We were just pieces in a game that had to be moved from A to B and he got paid for it. He was a mercenary, and I despised him for it.

He spoke to Blondie, myself and the two RAF boys, although I had to wait for Blondie to translate for me. We would be leaving the following day, he said. On to another safehouse, no doubt. Then Blondie added, 'We're being taken to the town of Perpignan at the foot of the Pyrenees.' A flash of excitement ran through me. 'Then it's over the mountains with a couple of guides, into Spain and through to Gibraltar.'

It was a happy moment. Banishing all thoughts of the difficulties we might face, we could only think of getting out of France and heading for home.

That night I lay awake, too excited, too full of thoughts, too aware of the dangers we had survived, and trying not to wonder if I would survive those that lay ahead. The only concrete thought in my head was that we would soon be on safe soil. And that's what kept my head buzzing throughout the night, as I lay upon my mattress wishing for neither sleep, nor great wealth, nor anything in the world but freedom.

It seemed as though the night would never end. Finally the sun rose, bringing the day when we would set off on the last leg of our journey. No one was more eager than I to get going. There was no sadness in saying goodbye to the Martins, their daughters or Edit. We had two guides now, one to accompany Blondie and myself to the station, and the other to bring along the RAF boys and de Merode. I was unhappy about having the Belgian prince along. I felt he would be trouble and I was not wrong.

This time our train had separate compartments joined by a long corridor, so we were all able to get in one compartment together. The journey and the lack of rest the night before made me sleepy; I began to doze off into a drifting, uneasy state. It was abruptly ended by a sharp dig in the ribs. Blondie said I was talking in my sleep. I drifted off again, and again I was woken by Blondie's elbow.

'Am I talking again?' He nodded. 'What was I saying?'

'I don't know exactly, but it was enough to let anyone passing know you weren't French.'

I tried to stay awake after that, and drank in the beautiful views as we sped along the Mediterranean coast and through sunlit countryside that seemed totally unspoilt by war. And then came the most breathtaking sight of all: the Pyrenees looming up, ominous, bleak and formidable.

Arriving at Perpignan we disembarked; that would be my last train ride through France and I was glad of it. As expected, German troops waited at the barrier. This was the nearest town to the Pyrenees and we expected the checking to be stringent. But when we showed our identity cards we passed through with no trouble.

Our escorts led the five of us to a roadside café where we found a table on the patio. The mountains beyond were inviting and I began to feel that safety was almost within reach. But danger was never far away, even now, for just a few yards from us sat a party of German officers. Our escorts ordered drinks and we sat and chatted, or rather the guides did; my contribution was to look innocent and unconcerned. An idle word now would bring this particular escape to a rapid and premature conclusion.

I kept one eye on the German officers who talked and laughed and seemed completely oblivious to us. Had we been armed Resistance fighters they would have been sitting ducks. And if we were to betray ourselves in any way, we would be the sitting ducks. We were so close to freedom now, that to be captured at this stage would be a cruel twist.

We waited at the café for an hour until a rickety old van passed by that the escorts recognized. We rose and made our way around the corner. The van was waiting for us. We climbed inside and then the van rumbled off, out of the village and up a gradually rising bumpy road. The higher we went the colder it got. Eventually the van stopped and we stepped out to be met by a most astonishing and unforgettable sight. Above us rose the towering mountains, snow-covered, awesome and magnificent; the only barrier between us and freedom.

We should wait here, we were told. Our guides would arrive shortly. Our escorts climbed back into the van and drove away.

We sat down to wait. The day wore on. Dusk fell. No one came.

'Well,' Blondie said at long last, 'it seems to me that we may have to make the rest of the journey on our own.'

We certainly weren't going to give in at this stage of the game. Of the five of us, Major Hasler was the ranking officer, much, I suspect, to the chagrin of Werner de Merode who probably felt he should be in charge. For my part, I would have followed the Major anywhere, despite the fact that all he had to help us find our way was a small compass.

We prepared to set off when there suddenly appeared a group of men. Two of them were swarthy, unshaven men wearing berets – clearly Basques. With them were two other men, one a Belgian flier and the other an Italian colonel.

The Colonel had absconded with a number of secret papers: good for you, I thought when I learned this. The young Belgian flier said he had been shot down. They were both as anxious as the rest of us to get going.

But what we didn't know was that the young Belgian was no escapee at all. He was not even Belgian. He was a German agent who had infiltrated the escape organization.

The Basques handed us each a parcel which contained a sweet potato and a pair of rope-soled shoes with canvas uppers. The shoes were essential for the crossing, they assured us.

'Blimey, they don't look like they'll last half an hour,' I said.

'I suggest you do as the man says,' the Major rebuked me.

He was right. The Basques were in charge and seemed to know what they were doing. In time they would prove to be not quite as sharp as we had imagined.

There was to be no talking whatsoever, they ordered. And then we began to walk towards the foot of the mountains that loomed up in the darkness. The air was cold and before long we were treading through ankle-deep snow. We came to the foot of the mountains and the climb became steeper.

'Everyone, walk in single file,' said a guard. 'Follow in each other's footsteps. That way you will not get lost.'

We filtered into single file and tramped along. I began to suffer the drain on strength that comes with high altitudes. In our group, the Major and I were in poorest shape, and I began to wonder how I would continue. But there was no turning back; nowhere to go but on and up, whatever the consequences.

We found ourselves wading through snow that reached our knees. It was freezing, but the sheer effort of traipsing through the deep snow brought on a heavy sweat. Compounding the physical exertion was shortness of breath and a terrible thirst. The Major and I panted heavily, fighting for the oxygen that grew thinner the higher we climbed, and soon we began to fall behind.

There was a short respite when we came to a deep ravine; the Major and I were able to catch up as the guides considered the rickety bridge strung across. The greatest danger came from a small cabin on the other side, close to the bridge. That was a patrol point, one of the guides explained. The German patrol housed inside was there precisely to catch people like us.

The young Belgian was neither as surprised by the discovery of the cabin nor as alarmed as we were. He must have considered how this could be his opportunity. As for the rest of us, we had no intention of getting captured by the Germans now.

The lights in the cabin were on; they were at home. But the guides decided we could make it. One by one we crossed the bridge, moving as quickly and stealthily as we could. A wrong move or sound would bring the patrol out of the cabin. As each man crossed, our hopes rose; the Germans remained unaware of our presence.

At any moment the young Belgian could have alerted the patrol. Why he chose not to do so remains obscure; I can only assume that he feared that his betrayal would have us killing him before the Germans got to us.

We all made it across and now the climb became even steeper. The snow got deeper and the air became painfully thin. My breath came in short gasps. I was soaked with perspiration and my tongue was so dry I felt sure it would swell and choke me. Blondie was becoming just as distressed. We decided to try eating snow. I placed some in my mouth and allowed it to melt. Its chill crispness was refreshing and I immediately felt better. I was better able to struggle on, stopping less frequently. Blondie fared better as well.

We climbed on through the night, resting only occasionally, trying to cover as much distance as possible before dawn. The snow came up to our waists.

Light gradually began to break through and we stopped to rest for half an hour. Then we began climbing again. The snow was now chest-deep. Progress was slow, laborious and tortuous. I gasped for breath, stopping now and again, trying fruitlessly to recover. My only relief was to eat snow. It would have been easy to give up, but no one and nothing was going to stop me from making it to freedom; not now. I went on, gasping, sweating and hurting.

Gradually the snow became more shallow and rocks appeared dotted about on the mountain side. Suddenly there came a warning from one of the guides. 'German patrol. Get down!'

We dropped virtually where we stood, taking cover behind rocks where there were some, keeping absolutely still; in that vast area of snow and rocks, one tiny movement would have been visible from miles away. Far ahead I could see the ski patrol; only the fact that they moved made it possible for me to see the white-camouflaged figures against the snow-covered slopes. If the young Belgian made any gesture to attract the Germans' attention, the patrol didn't see it. When the danger had passed we went on.

Up ahead a slight disagreement was ensuing between our two guides. They were arguing about which way to go. This did not bode well for us, since our lives were totally in their hands. I was beginning to realize that not even Blondie could have found his way over these mountains. The sky was overcast and bleak. The landscape was a series of peaks and valleys and finding ourselves lost within these huge ripples made it impossible to see more than a mile in any direction.

Halfway through the day the young Belgian said, to my surprise, 'We will soon be across the border.' The fact that he could gauge this, even though there were no visible signs of any frontier line between France and Spain, struck me as rather odd. But we were only too pleased that somebody seemed to know where we were, since the guides could still not agree on our whereabouts. As they continued to stop and argue, we were happy that the young Belgian had joined the guides in the lead. But then I began to wonder how it was that he knew so much about these mountains.

When the opportunity came, I took Blondie aside for a word. I was a bit puzzled about the young Belgian, I said. 'He seems to know his way very well. Seems a bit suspicious.'

Blondie agreed. 'I get the feeling that something's wrong with him, too. I think we'd better keep an eye on him.'

Even our Basque guides were now becoming suspicious of the young Belgian, and when they had the chance they related their concerns to the Major. One suggested we throw him off the mountain.

Blondie thought for a while. 'We don't know for sure if he is an agent,' he said. 'He doesn't seem to be an immediate threat. But the moment he does, we dispose of him.'

We trudged wearily on throughout the afternoon. Then came another warning — another German patrol. We dropped down, hardly daring to breathe. I found myself wondering about the young Belgian; had he seen the patrol but said nothing? I watched him for any sign of betrayal while we waited for the German patrol to pass out of sight. I was ready, as were the Basques no doubt, to ensure that if he made any sound to bring the Germans down on our heads, it would be the last sound he ever made. But by now he may have known that we were on to him. He had all but given himself away by sharing his knowledge of the mountains. He stayed still and silent, probably now valuing his own life above ours. Thus we evaded the enemy again.

Night was welcome when it came, allowing us to stop, taking shelter in a cave. We had covered around ten miles, though it felt more like sixty miles to me. It was bitterly cold but we were able to light a small fire over which we roasted sausages. Our spirits were high, despite the hardship. We were now across the border and into Spain.

We were up at dawn and set off again, now close to the top, 8,000 feet up. The snow was far more shallow and the gradient less steep. I was better able to keep up with the others, but still I lagged behind, although I was determined that nobody would have to stop and wait for me.

It was de Merode who decided he would hang back and wait. When I reached him, he berated me for being so slow. 'You're a disgrace to your regiment,' he finished.

Anger boiled up inside me, shaking off any remnant of exhaustion. I'd just about had enough of this Belgian twat. I looked to one side; there was a deep drop, a long way for a Belgian to fall, I thought.

'You say one more word to me and I'm going to throw you right over the top.'

He considered this for a moment, then swung about and shouted, 'Major Hasler!' Blondie stopped and turned. 'This private is threatening me,' said de Merode.

Blondie traipsed back and asked what the trouble was.

Before the Prince could speak I told Blondie to keep him off my back. 'I'm doing all right. I know where I'm going and I'm doing it at my pace, not his.'

Blondie faced the Belgian full on. 'I suggest you leave Bill alone,' he said. 'Now get up to the front, and stay there.'

De Merode walked on in a huff. Evening began to fall. The grey, overcast day turned quickly into a pitch-black night. The guides called for a halt and one of them told us to look back towards France. We did, and saw nothing but inky blackness. Then he took us around a bend and said, 'Now look.'

Spread out before us were the lights of Spain; millions of twinkling dots.

We just stood and looked, awestruck by the view. Then, without a word from anyone, the RAF boys, Blondie and I were running down towards the lights, suddenly drunk with joy, laughing, yelping, falling over, rolling down, not caring any longer, for now we were free of German-occupied territory, and ahead of us lay only freedom. Or internment, as the Basques were quick to remind us.

'You must wait,' they shouted. 'There will be Spanish police patrolling. If you're caught you will be interned.'

That was enough to bring us up short. The Spanish police were unpredictable. If they caught us they might hand us over to the Germans, or they might have us interned. Spanish internment camps were horrific. A lot of our boys who got across were lulled into a false sense of security, as we nearly were, and thinking they were safe, gave themselves up to the Spanish. They ended up in the internment camps, often for up to fifteen months before the British Consul was able to get them out. I heard of a camp that had only one water tap between hundreds of men. Toilet facilities were practically nonexistent. When our lads left those camps they were alive with lice and had to have their heads shaved. You were better off in a German POW camp. Now that we were free of German patrols, we had to be just as cautious of the Spanish ones.

We stopped for the night and continued the next day. Finally we left the snow behind us and were trekking down rock-strewn slopes. We were coming into Moorish country, one of the guides said. They suggested we should rest up for a day or two.

I was all for this rest business but I hadn't bargained for the kind of resting place the guides decided upon. It was a cave which smelt more like a zoo, for it was occupied by a family of Moors and their sheep and goats and donkeys.

We settled down to eat sweet potato and drink some rough wine. 'It's so dark in here,' I said to Blondie, 'I don't know if I'm sitting on straw or a pile of donkey shit.'

The Moors sat opposite, looking at us and muttering among themselves. I didn't like the look of them at all. They looked like the type that, if they heard a couple of coins tinkling in your pockets, would cut your head off. Not the sort of people you'd take to tea with the vicar.

At least the cave was dry and warm. I was relieved when, after several hours, the guides announced we were to continue. I was happy to see the last of the Moors and their sheep, goats and donkeys. It was good to step outside and breathe in fresh air once more, Spanish air at that. France was now a memory, and provided we could make it through Spain and into Gibraltar, England would be just a plane or a boat ride away.

9

THE PYRENEES WERE NOW BEHIND US. We had reached the foot of the mountains on the Spanish side. We were well stocked up with sweet potatoes given to us by the Basques and oranges supplied by the Moors. Ahead lay a road littered with stones and small rocks, along which much traffic was unlikely to go. Walking along in daylight should prove no great risk, although there might be patrols of Spanish policemen.

Jack Dawson was having problems of his own. De Merode had given him a dressing down and Jack dropped back, looking worried. 'What's the matter, mate?' I asked.

'It's that Belgian pig. He's going to bloody well report me when we get back,' Jack said. 'He's taken my name and number and he's going to put me on report. I'm due for promotion, but if he puts me on report I won't get it.'

Jack insisted that he'd done nothing at all to warrant this severity. I was indignant, and mentioned it to Blondie. He heard me out and then listened to Jack. Then he marched smartly along until he had caught up with de Merode.

'What's all this about you putting Jack Dawson on report?' Blondie said, speaking almost informally, one officer to another.

'I do not have to give my reasons to you. I am Dawson's superior officer and....'

Blondie interrupted him, his tone now authoritative, a tinge of anger beneath the surface. 'Listen here, you pack this up. *I'm* in charge here. *I'm* the senior officer, understand? There will be no reporting anyone unless I say so. Now I want you to show me Jack's name and number.' De Merode was taken aback by Blondie's outburst. If de Merode had mistaken the Major's usual calm demeanour to mean weakness he now knew he was very much mistaken. Sheepishly, de Merode took out his pad in which he had written Jack's details and showed it to Blondie. 'Tear it up,' the Major ordered. De Merode tore the page from his pad and ripped it up while Blondie looked coolly on. Then, after a few choice words to the Belgian prince, Blondie recovered his calm and moved away.

Further on down the road, one of the guides stopped and said, 'Police.' And there they were, a group of Spanish policemen, not far ahead of us, coming our way. This was not like it was in the mountains when the patrol was spotted miles off. These policemen were only a matter of several hundred yards away so that even I could see them. And they must have seen us.

We scattered, leaving the road and taking cover behind large rocks and boulders. Not even the young Belgian wanted to be taken by them. The patrol came nearer, the policemen talking and smoking cigarettes, seemingly unaware of us even though I could have sworn they had seen us. They strolled on by, and we simply had to wait until they were far enough away for us to emerge from behind the rocks.

Probably they had seen us. But whether they felt sorry for us, or simply could not be bothered with us, we would never know.

We carried on down the road and from time to time we saw other patrols, and each time as we took cover they passed us by. I could not believe our luck. If it would just hold out a little longer... Even the young Belgian who had aroused our suspicions was less of a threat now.

At length we came to a small house standing on its own beside the road. We could rest here, one of the Basques told us. We went inside and were greeted by a very jovial Spaniard who was no doubt being very well paid by the organization to provide such cordiality. The house was extremely comfortable, more like a small hotel, except that we were the only guests. Not that I could imagine anyone making reservations there as it was miles from anywhere. It was obviously set up purely as part of the escape organization. Our rooms seemed most luxurious and the beds were soft and clean. I fell onto my bed and slept like a baby through the night. Meanwhile, our guides had disappeared.

It was strange to wake up in the morning with a roof over my head yet no longer to be in France. I rose, washed and found that the patrón had prepared a superb breakfast for us, with real eggs. This was luxury indeed. The owner couldn't do enough for us, seeing to our every need and making sure we were well fed.

It was tempting at this stage to think that the ordeal was over. But

I tried to suppress such thoughts for the Spanish patrols, even though they had appeared uninterested in us, were still a major threat. I decided that I would not feel safe until I was in Gibraltar.

After a few days our guides returned. It was time to go on again. Sixty miles away lay Barcelona; this time, though, we would not be walking. Our guides had arranged for a lorry to take us. It duly arrived, loaded up with toilet seats and packing straw. Daylight was fast fading as we climbed in, hiding behind the toilet seats and making ourselves as comfortable as possible among all the straw. The lorry shunted into gear and we rattled off, the toilet seats shaking all around us.

About an hour later we came to a halt. We were at a checkpoint. Shrinking even further back behind the toilet seats, we tried to draw the straw around us, to make us completely invisible.

The tailboard was dropped open. It was pitch dark outside. A torch shone in, sweeping over what appeared to be nothing but a pile of toilet seats. Suddenly my eyes were blinded as the torch shone straight in my face. I blinked, trying not to shift my position. The light lingered. The policeman had seen me. Then the torch was switched off and the policeman stepped away. Moments passed. The tailboard slammed shut. The lorry again shunted forward; we had passed through the checkpoint.

That was one policeman who must have been well paid by the escape organization for turning a blind eye.

It was the early hours of the morning and still dark when we pulled into Barcelona and the lorry finally came to a stop. We climbed out and followed our guides through brilliantly lit streets, a sight that was strange after the blackout of Britain and France. Eventually we came to an old hotel or lodging house where rooms had been prepared for us. We were to spend another night in comfort and luxury. I hoped that this was the shape of things to come. I for one had no trouble sleeping, wakened only in the morning by an incessant knocking at the door.

Oh my God, the police! That was my first thought. I slipped out of bed, wondering if, after all this, I was about to be arrested. I unlocked the door and opened it, hardly daring to look at who or what waited outside.

There stood a uniformed chauffeur. 'Good morning, sir,' he said in English. 'I have come to take you to the British Consulate.'

It took a moment or two for his words to sink in. I wanted to laugh out loud, but stifled it.

I rushed about, washing and dressing, and by the time I was ready the chauffeur had roused Blondie. Outside waited a huge car, a Union Jack perched on its bonnet — a beautiful sight. I could hardly believe that the worst of the ordeal was now over. Yet even now I retained a certain sense of caution, aware that I still had to get to Gibraltar. Blondie and I climbed in and we were swiftly driven to the British Consulate.

The British Vice Consul himself welcomed us, and gave his regrets that it was necessary for us to be questioned at length. We were ushered into a room where we were questioned at length by such a cynical young Intelligence officer that it turned into an interrogation. He seemed to have a great deal of trouble believing that we were English, let alone survivors from Operation Frankton.

The problem was that large numbers of men escaping from France were seeking help from the British Embassy in Madrid. Only a few of them were escaping British servicemen; most were French who claimed to be French-Canadian — the French Embassy sent their countrymen straight back to France. A transit camp had been set up for these escapees, from where those who proved to be genuinely French-Canadian were sent to Britain. Otherwise they were dispatched to a Free French district in North Africa.

Finally convincing our interrogator that we were genuine British Marines, we rejoined the Vice Consul. He told us that if we were discovered by the authorities we would be interned, so we were not entirely out of the woods yet. For now we would remain here at the Consulate until arrangements were made to get us to Madrid and then Gibraltar. 'My wife and I will be glad to have you both as our guests,' he finished warmly.

Our stay with the Vice Consul and his wife was a joyous time. We could now relax and take advantage of all the luxuries the Consulate offered. We were allowed to write a letter home which would be sent in a diplomatic bag, although the Vice Consul said he would have to censor the contents, of course.

During our stay, word came that the young Belgian had mysteriously disappeared instead of seeking refuge as did the rest of us. By now he would have blown the whistle on part if not all of the escape organization. 'The people I worry about the most,' said

Blondie, 'are the men, women and children who gave us refuge. What will happen to them if he is able to reveal their involvement? They are the real heroes.'

What happened to de Merode and, more to the point, the two RAF lads, I never knew, but they were undoubtedly cared for. I had promised Jack that we would meet up again later in England, but I never saw him again.

A few days later the Vice Consul came to us and said he was going to drive us to Madrid himself. 'We're leaving today, so gather your things.'

It was somewhat comforting to be travelling through Spain in an embassy car with the Vice Consul himself, as the likelihood of being stopped was virtually nil. It was a long and tedious journey, thankfully unexciting, with nothing more to do than enjoy the views.

We arrived in Madrid as dusk was settling. We passed through the giant gates of the British Embassy, and as we did we received a salute from the Spanish policemen on duty there. That seemed strange to me, considering that the Spanish police would have interned me if I had been caught. Inside, I was shown to a small but comfortable room which would be my own private quarters during my stay there.

Because Major Hasler had thinning hair and a moustache and looked much older than his years, it was decided that he could claim to be beyond military age — only British men of military age were interned — and so he was able to obtain a police pass as a commercial traveller. He then spent much of his time outside the Consulate, walking the streets freely and eventually moving into a hotel.

I was now alone and missed the Major, but two days later I was joined at the Embassy by two RAF boys. Their arrival cheered me up and they taught me the rudiments of bridge, although I never mastered the game. They, on the other hand, were experts, so I never stood a chance; but they were good company.

One day we were wandering around the grounds when one of the Spanish guards told us there was a funeral at the German Embassy opposite. The German attaché had died on the operating table while having his appendix removed.

I said to the lads, 'I think we ought to watch that, don't you?' So we went down to the gates, and as the funeral procession passed us we stood cheering and laughing: *'Hooray! Ha! Ha! Ha!'* It was one of the highlights of my stay there.

Lieutenant Mackinnon and James Conway were led out of their cells at the Gestapo headquarters in Paris and escorted into a courtyard. Bloodstains were splattered on one of the walls. The firing squad lined up. The officer in charge carried out his orders without compunction. On the command, the squad aimed — and fired.

Next came two more British Marines, Petty Officer Laver and Bill Mills. Neither they nor Mackinnon or Conway said anything to betray Blondie and myself. They were the bravest of men.

Weeks later, Conway's mother received through the Red Cross a message that said both Conway and Mackinnon were prisoners. It continued, 'Have seen James last week. He is healthy and conveys New Year's greetings to you. Don't worry.'

It had taken three months for the message to get through.

Around the same time, Moffat's mother received a telegram notifying her that her boy's body was reported to have been found washed ashore on 17 December. Mountbatten wrote her a personal letter of sympathy.

Towards the end of March Blondie came to me and said he had been offered a flight home: 'I think I shall take it,' he said.

It was hard to believe that suddenly Blondie and I were to be parted. But I was happy for him. 'Fine,' I said. 'I'll see you when I get back.'

He was going because he was considered to be 'utmost priority'. I was considered a lesser priority. However, the day did come when I left the Embassy and headed, at long last, for the Rock of Gibraltar.

I travelled from Madrid by train, which took me to the border station. From there it was just a short walk. Ahead of me I could see Gibraltar. Once there, I would be totally safe, but first I had to go through a checkpoint manned by the Spanish. I marched eagerly towards it, passed the Spanish guards without challenge, and came at last to the British checkpoint. I was on British soil.

'Identification card, please.' The British MP sounded very businesslike.

I was nonplussed for a moment, but with a friendly smile I said,

'I'm English, mate, like you. I've just escaped from France. I don't have any identification.'

'No identification?' he roared. 'Put this man under arrest!'

I had avoided the gendarmes, the Germans and Spanish, only to be arrested by the British. I could not believe it.

I was marched round to a small building and taken inside, where a MI5 officer proceeded to interrogate me.

'Who are you? What is your unit? What were you doing in France? You have no identification; how do we know you're telling us the truth? Marine Sparks may be lying dead somewhere with a German bullet in him.'

I was still under suspicion because there were occasions when the Germans made it even this far through the system.

Obviously my answers didn't satisfy MI5 and I remained under arrest, kept on board the ship *Cormorant* under close scrutiny and in seclusion. While scanning through the marines' daily orders, I found to my horror that I had been posted missing, presumed killed. Almost certainly my father would have received a telegram to that effect. I had to figure out a way of getting home. But for now I was under lock and key, unable to convince MI5 or the Military Police that I was indeed Marine Sparks.

It turned out that Blondie, despite being rushed back to England, had also had trouble proving himself to be *the* Major Hasler. Various security men had questioned him during his journey home, but he remained suspect until friends at COHQ finally confirmed his identity.

A few days later I was taken under guard to a waiting boat and ferried out to a waiting troopship. There I was kept in isolation in a small cabin on the upper deck, away from the other passengers. I spent the whole voyage there, having my food brought to me. We docked in Liverpool and all passengers disembarked except me. I was moved to another cabin where I was interrogated again by another MI5 agent. 'Who are you? What is your unit?...'

Still under escort, I was taken down to the dock gates and handed over to the Military Police. 'This man is to be put on a train for London and the door to his compartment locked,' the MPs were told. 'You, Sparks, will be met at Euston by the Military Police and you'll be taken to the Euston Hotel for further interrogation.'

I was thoroughly miserable now and could think of nothing more but getting home to my father. The red-caps stood on the platform, keeping their eyes on me until the train pulled out. The journey lasted through the night. I was becoming desperate to go to the toilet, but I was locked in. Through some seemingly futile sense of desperation I tried the door. It opened. The red-caps had forgotten to lock it. I went out into the corridor and made my way down to the toilet, then went for a stroll up and down the corridor.

It was barely dawn as we pulled into Euston. On the platform stood two red-caps on the lookout for somebody, presumably me. I shot down the corridor and disembarked along with everybody else. The red-caps boarded the train and began searching the compartments. While I passed through the ticket barrier the red-caps must have been wondering why they could find no locked door with a prisoner behind it. Before they could figure out that I was not on the train at all, I was down the underground and heading for Finsbury Park.

I arrived at Dad's door and knocked. It was very early in the morning. Dad opened the door cautiously, wondering who was knocking him up at such a time. Then he laid eyes on me.

'Bill!' he yelled with unbelieving delight, and threw his arms around me. 'We thought you dead, boy. Oh, Bill, I can't believe it, God, I'm so thankful, so happy to see you.'

My stepmother appeared, wondering what all the noise was about, and joined Dad in hugging and kissing me. It was one of the happiest moments of my life.

10

I REMAINED HOME FOR TWO DAYS, ignoring the order to report to the Euston Hotel. I felt it was far more important that my parents had this time with me, so after spending two days assuring them that I had come back alive and well, I caught the bus to Euston and entered the hotel.

There stood a sergeant major, an Army man. I resented talking to the Army as we considered them junior to us. But I went up to him and said, 'I'm supposed to report here.'

He eyed me, 'Who are you, lad?'

'Marine Sparks, Sarg Major.'

'What?' he roared, then in his best parade voice, 'Escort!' I thought: Oh Christ, here we go again.

A soldier quickly appeared. 'Take this man upstairs,' the sergeant major bellowed, and I was hastily marched up and into a room. There I remained for an hour or so under guard and finally was taken into another office. There, to my relief, sat a Naval Intelligence officer.

He looked up at my Army guard and said, 'What are you supposed to be?'

'Escort, sir.'

'Escort? What for?'

'This man's been absent, sir.'

'Right, outside.' My escort left. The officer looked up at me and said, 'Who are you?'

'Marine Sparks, sir.'

'Now what the bloody hell have you been doing?'

'I'd been reported missing, presumed dead, so I went home first to let my family know that I was still alive, sir.'

'That sounds reasonable, Sparks. When was this?'

'Two days ago, sir.'

'Dear oh dear, you naughty boy. That doesn't sound quite so reasonable. Perhaps you had better explain everything to me.' And so, in the briefest possible terms, I gave him a rundown of the operation and our escape through France.

After listening to my story he said, 'Somehow you've got to get round to Combined Ops HQ at Richmond Terrace in Whitehall. Just suppose that while I'm looking through this filing cabinet, you went out that other door. Do you think you could find your way to Richmond Terrace?'

'Yes, sir.'

'Very good. And leave your friend out there.'

He got out of his chair and went over to the filing cabinet. While his back was turned, I shot out through the other door and hightailed it to COHQ, wondering what kind of reception I would find there.

I arrived to find I was expected. Everyone came out to welcome me. Even colonels were there to say, 'Well, well, Sparks, welcome home. You have done a fine job. Well done.'

I was then told to get myself back down to Southsea, and wasted no time obeying this order. I caught the train to Portsmouth and bussed it to Southsea — I had come home. It was now summer, almost a year since I first arrived in Southsea and some six months since the operation.

Blondie was waiting for me. It was a happy reunion, but I felt angry at the way I had been treated since reaching Gibraltar. I said, 'It bloody well annoys me, all those months in occupied-bloody-France, going through Spain and I don't get arrested until setting foot in friendly territory.'

He laughed and said. 'Just goes to show how good our security is.'

I had to admit he'd got a good point there.

Shortly after I got back, I called round to White Heather to visit Mrs Powell and Heather. But only Mrs Powell was there. Heather was in hospital with TB, she told me. Then she explained that, some time after we had left on our mission, Heather had had a premonition that Jock Ewart, her Bob, was not coming back, and she had been so traumatized by this that she had gone into rapid TB.

I went to see her in hospital the next day. She was weak, unwilling to fight her illness. It was heartbreaking to see. She had loved Jock so much, more than any of us had realized.

She said to me, 'Bobby's not coming back, is he?'

'Of course he is,' I told her with a confident smile. 'He'll be following me along soon.'

'No,' she said, 'I'm sorry, but he's not coming back.' Nothing I could say would give her hope, no matter how slim that hope was.

Some time later she was allowed home. Her father would soon be back from the sea in time for her seventeenth birthday. But he arrived too late. Heather died just a month before her birthday.

Later, we learned that Ewart, along with Wallace, had been executed on the night we accomplished our operation. They had been interrogated with 'no methods barred' — a term I cannot forget. Yet they never revealed anything, allowing us to finish the job. If anyone deserved the Victoria Cross, they did. But they didn't get it.

One day Blondie, now a Colonel, had me report to his office. 'Congratulations,' he said, 'You have been awarded the DSM, and very well earned.' It was a tremendous honour and I was immensely proud. I received my medal at Buckingham Palace, presented to me by His Majesty King George VI. Blondie received the DSO.

I was distressed, though, that the other lads — those who had died in the course of their duty — had received no medals. However, collectively we became known as the 'Cockleshell Heroes.'

On 12 January, 1944, a German staff officer, Major Reichel, signed a document which purported to show what treatment was given to various prisoners. This was used as propaganda for the defence during the Russian trials held in Kharkov where Nazi officers were tried for war crimes. It contained a portion concerning Operation Frankton, including an accusation that we who had taken part had committed atrocities. In part it reported that

> Of the ten who took part in the attack, the following were captured a few days later:
>
> Mackinnon, Naval Lieutenant, born 15.7.21, North Argyllshire.
>
> Laver, Albert Friedrich, Petty Officer, born 29.9.20, Birkenhead.
>
> Mills, William Henri, Marine, born 15.12.21, Kettering.
>
> Wallace, Samuel, Sergeant, born 24.9.13, Dublin, Eire.
>
> Conway, James, Marine, born 28.8.22, Stockport.
>
> Ewart, Robert, Marine, born 4.12.21, Glasgow.
>
> A seventh soldier, Moffat, was found drowned. The rest,

among them their leader, Major Hasler, Marine Sparks and Corporal Sheard, presumably escaped to Spain.

Sheard's body had never been found. Some have theorized that he did manage to escape, making it to the Channel Islands. It's a theory I would like to believe, but if he did survive he has never made himself known, and it must be assumed that he did in fact drown. The report went on with the barefaced lie that we were 'wearing special olive-grey garments without any military badges . . . Noteworthy punishable offences committed on their flight have not been discovered up till now.'

For the killings of Wallace and Ewart, Colonel von Tippelskirch was brought to trial in 1948 in Hamburg. Admiral Buchmann should have stood with him but he was reported dead. Lieutenant Theodor Prahm, who personally supervised the execution of Wallace and Ewart, took the stand as a witness. He was unable to confirm any order being given to him to carry out the execution, and Judge-Advocate Mr C. L. Stirling KC told him, 'You brought the German Navy into complete and everlasting disrepute by this monstrous thing.'

The trial dragged on from August until October. Von Tippelskirch was acquitted. No other members of the German Navy were indicted for the bloody deed.

After the war I was called in by COHQ and told by the Sergeant Major that there had been two more awards given. Laver and Mills had been 'Mentioned in Despatches'.

I was furious. Those two men had given their lives. At least they should have received DSMs.

It wasn't possible to award them DSMs, I was told. The only medal that could be awarded posthumously was the Victoria Cross.

I said, 'So give it to them. The boys did their job. They gave their lives. What more do you want?'

'The Victoria Cross can only be given when the deed has been witnessed by a senior officer.'

Who could have been there watching them do their job? I was stunned and angry. I told the Sergeant Major, 'Right, then you can have my DSM back.'

The Sergeant Major blew his top, saying that I was insulting the Crown.

I thought then that from that moment on I would do everything I could to see that all the lads who gave their lives in that operation received due recognition. I found myself up against miles of British red tape but I was determined not to give up. I made my protests at every opportunity and more than once I was told in no uncertain terms to forget the idea completely. That made me all the more determined to continue. The years and the decades passed away.

I collected signatures and petitioned various Members of Parliament, but was always told that nothing could be done. I eventually appealed to the Queen. I received a letter from her secretary regretting that Her Majesty could not interfere. I am sure that the Queen never even got to see my letter.

After exhausting every avenue I could think of, I decided that if the British Government would not honour those lads, I would appeal to the French Government and hopefully obtain French decorations for them. But I was informed that, if the French authorities agreed to award the men, the British Government was entitled to refused any such awards.

In desperation, I called upon my Member of Parliament, Sir Bernard Braine. A wonderful man, he immediately took up the cudgels and entered the fight personally. He became like a little terrier; once he got his teeth into something he wouldn't let go. He gained support from other MPs and managed to open files that had been locked away for ever.

One day Sir Bernard phoned me. He'd been thinking, he said. 'If we do manage to get medals for the boys, obviously they're not all going to be the same grade medals, and then we're going to have their parents wanting to know why. Don't you think it would be better if we built a monument to all of them?'

On reflection I agreed.

We organized a fund in the *Daily Telegraph* and the response was so terrific that within a month we had enough money to build the memorial. It was erected in the barracks of the Royal Marines Special Boats Squadron and unveiled by Sir Steuart Pringle, Commandant General, Royal Marines, in 1983.

As the memorial was revealed to my eyes for the first time, I discovered that my own name had been included on the stone. At first, I was horrified.

'I'm not dead yet,' I told Sir Bernard. 'It's like looking at your own name on a tombstone.'

He replied rather wryly, 'Well, you're not going to live forever and when you are gone, nobody's going to come down and add your name to the list. So I had it put on.'

I could see he was right, and I was grateful. It was a proud and moving moment that day. It had taken thirty-eight years to achieve this.

And yet as I stood there remembering those boys — the trials we went through and the laughs we had during our training; the disastrous beginning to the operation when we lost two crews in the tidal races; the loss of our third canoe which became separated from us and went on valiantly alone; the feeling of euphoria after we had planted our mines; the knowledge that, while we didn't sink as many ships as we'd hoped to, we did cause damage, chaos and confusion; the long trek through France; and more than anything else, the incredible courage and unbreakable spirit of all my companions who had come to be known as the Cockleshell Heroes, I felt that those who had gone — Lieutenant Mackinnon, Corporal Sheard, Sergeant Wallace, Corporal Laver, Bill Mills, David Moffat, Jock Ewart and James Conway — were all there with me. Even as I write, and with Blondie Hasler now gone, although I am the last of the Cockleshell Heroes I am never without the others.

It was 30 June, 1988. I stood at the rear of Sotheby's auction rooms with Rene, my wife. The auctioneer was addressing the audience.

'Gentlemen, we will start at four thousand.'

Only £4,000 for my medal, I thought with some alarm. What on earth did this man think he was doing? But then I hadn't had much experience with auctions, and I was much relieved when I watched hands acknowledging the bids which rose at an alarming rate.

'Four thousand, five hundred ... Five thousand ... Five thousand, five hundred ... Six thousand ... '

I could not believe it as the bids passed the £12,000 mark. Then £15,000. £20,000. And still the bids kept coming.

My DSM medal was the main item for auction that day. As the bidding rose, so the number of bidders began to dwindle until there were only two left: a representative of the Royal Marines Museum and a telephone bidder who wished to remain anonymous.

The Royal Marines Museum made their final bid, £30,000.

'Thirty thousand. I have thirty thousand,' said the auctioneer. By now I was totally bewildered at the amount. Then the signal came that the telephone bidder had made a further bid. 'Thirty-one thousand.'

The Royal Marines Museum conceded defeat. The auctioneer's hammer finally fell. 'Sold at thirty-one thousand pounds.'

At first I felt as though I could weep with joy at the astronomical amount my medal had brought me. But then I was overcome with remorse at the loss of my medal.

'Come on,' said Rene, 'at least our home is safe.'

I managed a smile. After all, we had almost lost our home. Then what good would the medal have been, with no home to keep it in?

And so the medal was gone. Yet I still retained the initials DSM to follow my name, and, more importantly still, the memories of my comrades whose names were etched in the memorial raised in the barracks of the Royal Marines Special Boats Squadron.

We went home, looking forward to settling down to a quiet and peaceful life. In one way or another Operation Frankton, or Cockleshell, had not ended for me during the war. Now, at long last, I was ready to settle.

INDEX

Alabama, 68, 73
Al Rawdah, Indian merchant ship, 40
Arsenal Football Club, 17
Auschwitz, 115, 116

Barbie (daughter of Mary Lindell), 108
Barcelona, 135
Barnet, 35
Bassens South, 68
Bay of Biscay, 45, 49, 50, 52
Benzedrine, 62
Bilbao, 97
Birkenhead, 143
Birmingham, 25
Bismark, 2, 14, 15, 18, 35
Blackwall, 39
'Blanket', 38, 40, 46, 57
Blaye, 74, 80
Blitz, 3, 4, 6, 16-17
Bordeaux, 48, 58, 62, 66, 67-73, 80, 81, 83, 89, 92, 96, 112, 124
Boulogne, 48
Braine, Sir Bernard, 145-6
Brest, 67
British Intelligence, 76, 80, 85, 124, 125,136,139
Buchmann, Admiral, 58, 61, 67, 144
Bute Island, 41

Cachalot, 44, 51
Café de Paris, 46, 90
Carter, Mr, 114, 117-20
Catfish, 44, 51
Cessac, 96
Channel Islands, 144
Chelsea Football Club, 26
Cheyrau, Monsieur, 96
Chichester, 30
Churchill, Prime Minister Winston, 48, 63, 112
Clyde, 40
Coalfish, 44, 51, 53
Cockle Mark I, 33, 48

Cockle Mark II, 33, 39, 48
Cockle suit, 41
Combined Operations, 24, 40, 44, 47, 111, 112, 124, 139, 142, 144
Compact rations, 59
Conger, 44, 51, 53, 54
Conway, James, 35, 51, 53, 56, 66, 96-8, 111-12, 138, 143, 146
Courduan, 45
Crayfish, 44, 51, 56, 72, 125
Cuttlefish, 44, 51, 54, 56

Daily Telegraph, 145
Dawson, Jack, 123-4, 133, 137
Deal, 3, 24, 26, 30, 41
De Merode, Werner, 122, 125, 127, 130-1, 133-4, 137
Deptford, 38
Desert Island, 64
Devonshire, 35
Distinguished Service Medal, 1-2, 31, 143, 144, 146-7
Dresden, 73
Dublin, 28, 143
DuBois, Madame, 95, 98-100
DuBois, Monsieur, 95-6, 98-103
Dunkirk, 97

Eastney Barracks, 32, 33, 34
Edit, 122-5
Edwards, Sergeant W. J. 'Bungy', 23-5, 26
Eighth Army, 98
Ellery, Bill, 25, 26, 34, 51-2
Elizabeth II, Queen, 145
Ewart, Robert 'Jock', 25, 30, 32, 51, 53, 57, 58, 61, 64, 67, 72-3, 80, 142-3, 144, 146

Fisher, Eric, 25, 28, 29, 38, 51, 52
Fishermen at Pointe aux Oiseaux, 60-1
French Resistance, 46, 86-8, 93, 94, 116
Frontenac, 97

Garonne, 68

Gascony, 58
Gebauer, Captain Max, 58
Geneva Convention, 44, 58, 80
George VI, King, 1, 143
Gestapo, 67, 101, 103, 115, 122-3, 138
Gibraltar, 8, 9, 10, 13, 16, 125, 132, 136, 138
Gironde, 45, 52, 54, 67, 112
Glasgow, 25, 28, 143
Goatley, Fred, 48

Hamburg, 144
Hamilton, Marie, 124
Hasler, Major 'Blondie'
  Allowed to walk streets of Madrid, 137
  Assigned to Combined Operations, 47
  Attacks ships at Bordeaux, 69-72
  Begins escape bid with Sparks, 74
  Begins training of men in canoes, 28, 29
  Betrayed to gendarmes, 84-5
  Bids farewell to Laver and Mills, 72
  Bids farewell to Mary Lindell, 114, 115
  Cautions de Merode, 131, 133
  Childhood, 47
  Christmas with the DuBois family, 99, 100
  Chooses Sparks as his Number 2, 38
  Calm demeanour, 75, 82, 92, 98-9, 100
  Convinces Mountbatten to send him on
    mission, 47-8
  Decides to move training to Scotland, 40
  Designs Cockle Mark II with Fred Goatley,
    48
  Develops way to launch canoes from
    submarine, 42
  Disciplines Sparks, 36
  Disembarks from Tuna, 51
  Flies back from Spain, 138
  Given refuge by French, 83-4, 88, 92-3, 95,
    98-103, 112-13, 121-2
  Guided to Ruffec, 89-90
  Interrogated by Mary Lindell, 106-7
  Interviews Sparks, 21
  Leads men in 'Blanket' exercise, 39
  Leads way into tidal races, 52, 53
  Meets his commandos for the first time, 26
  Personal training in canoe, 47, 48
  Prepares to lead party over Pyrenees, 127
  Promoted to Colonel, 143
  Receives DSO, 143
  Refuses flight out of France ahead of Sparks,
    107
  Reveals 'Operation Frankton' to the men,
    45-6
  Scuttles Catfish, 74
  Selects twelve for 'Operation Frankton', 35
  Sends coded message to COHQ, 111, 112,
    124
  Taken to the line of demarcation, 93-5
  Writes paper on attacking methods, 47
Hideouts along the Gironde, 59, 62, 64, 65, 68
Hitler's Commando Order, 58, 80
HMS Ark Royal, 9, 10, 13-15
HMS Barham, 16
HMS Cormorant, 139
HMS Forth, 40
HMS Hood, 14, 15
HMS Naiad, 17, 20
HMS Prince of Wales, 14,15
HMS Renown, 2
  Attacked by Italian and German air forces,
    9, 12, 13
  Captures two armed German merchant ships,
    10
  Escorts convoy to Cape Town, 9-11
  Escorts convoys to Malta, 11, 12
  First action, 9
  Hit by enemy aircraft, 13
  Refit in Scotland, 16, 18
  Sea battle with Italian Navy, 12-13
  Search for the Bismark, 14-15
  Service for its dead, 13
  Stationed in Iceland, 18-19
HMS Rodney, 15
HMS Tuna, 44, 49-52, 124

Iceland, 18, 20
Ile de Cazeau, 64-5, 66, 68
Isle of Sheppey, 39
Isle of Wight, 26
Italian Air Force, 11-13
Italian Navy, 12-13, 20

Jaubert, Louis, 96-8, 111-12
Jaubert, Madame, 96-8, 111-12

Kettering, 35, 143
Kharkov, 143
King, Sergeant, 31

La Faye, 90
La Garde, 80

La Réole, 97-8,111, 112
Laver, Corporal, A. F., 35, 51, 53, 56, 62, 69, 72, 73, 80, 138, 143, 144, 146
Leros, raid on, 29, 31
Lindell, Mary (Marie-Claire), 96, 98, 100-3, 106-16, 119, 124
Limpet mine, 42-3, 48, 69-71
Liverpool, 139
London, 2, 3, 29, 30, 38, 40, 106, 123, 124
Luftwaffe, 2, 11, 12, 34, 57
Lumps Fort, 26
Lyons, 101, 103-5, 112

Mackinnon, Lieutenant Jack, 28-9, 39, 44, 46, 51, 53, 56, 66-7, 96-7, 98, 111-12, 138, 143, 146
Madrid, 136, 137, 138
Malta, 11, 12, 13
Maquis group, 86-8
Margate, 38, 39, 40
Marie-Claire (see Lindell, Mary)
Marseilles, 121-3
Martin, Madame, 122, 123, 125
Martin, Monsieur, 122, 123, 125,
Maurice (son of Mary Lindell), 101-6, 109-10 112-13, 118, 120
Medway, 39
Meisel, Rear-Admiral Wilhelm, 58
Mills, Bill, 35, 42, 51, 53, 56, 61, 62, 69, 72, 80, 143, 144, 146
Moffat, David, 25-6, 51, 53, 54, 58, 67, 138, 143, 146
Montgomery, General Sir Bernard L., 98
Mountbatten, Lord Louis, 24, 40, 47, 48, 112, 138

North Argyllshire, 143
Norway, 29, 45, 68

Paris, 58, 67, 80, 138
Pat, 125
Perpignan, 125, 126
Plymouth, 47, 67
Pointe aux Oiseaux, 60
Pointe de Grave, 45, 54, 57
Poland, 58, 67
Porte de Calogne, 62
Portland, 68, 73
Portsmouth, 23, 47, 61, 82, 142
Powell, Heather, 25, 32, 57, 142-3

Powell, Mrs, 25, 57, 142
Prahm, Lieutenant Theodor, 72-3, 144
Pringle, Sir Steuart, 145
Pusser's Rum, 55, 59, 82
Pyrenees, 125-32

Raikes, Captain, 49-51
Rais, 89-90
Reichel, Major, 143
Reykjavik, 18
Rommel, Field-Marshal Erwin, 98
Rosyth, 16, 18
Roumazières, 101, 103
Royal Marine Boom Patrol Detachment, 26, 31
Royan, 58, 67, 68
Ruffec, 46, 75, 82, 89, 90, 94

St Julien, 64
St Mème-les-Carrières, 80
Scapa Flow, 6-8, 19
Seaview, 26
Security Police, 67, 72, 80
Selborne, Lord, 48
Sheard, Corporal G. J., 35, 40, 51, 53-4 55, 58, 67, 144, 146
Signals School, 33
Somerville, Admiral Sir James, 9, 10, 12, 13, 14, 16
Sotheby's, 1, 146-7
Southsea, 22, 25, 31, 33, 39, 47, 69, 142
Southsea Stroll, 33
Spanish internment camps, 131
Sparks, Benny (older brother), 17-20, 73
Sparks, Irene (wife), 1, 2, 146, 147
Sparks, William
  Accident in Iceland, 18-19
  Arrested in Gibraltar, 139
  Arrives in Lyons, 104
  Arrives in Marseilles, 121
  Arrives in Spain, 131-3
  Attacks ships at Bordeaux, 69-72
  Auctions Distinguished Service Medal, 1, 2, 146-7
  Awarded Distinguished Service Medal, 143
  Becomes Hasler's Number 2, 38
  Begins escape bid, 74
  Betrayed to gendarmes, 84-5
  Bids farewell to Laver and Mills, 72
  Bids farewell to Mary Lindell, 114, 115

Campaign to have Cockleshell Heroes honoured, 144-6
Crosses the Pyrenees, 126-32
Detects German agent, 129-30
Disembarks from *Tuna*, 51
Endures U-boat attack in *Tuna*, 49-50
Experiences at Deal, 24-5, 26-7, 30-1, 40-1
First action aboard the *Renown*, 9
Given refuge by French, 83-4, 88, 92-3, 95, 98-103, 112-13, 121-2
Guided to Ruffec, 89-90
In abandoned house with Hasler, 119-20
Interrogated by British Intelligence, 136, 139
Joins Royal Marines, 2-3
Meets Hasler, 21
Meets Mary Lindell, 106
Parts from Hasler in Spain, 138
Reaction to 'Operation Frankton', 45, 46
Returns to England under guard, 139
Scuttles *Catfish*, 74
Scuttles *Conger*, 54
Separated from Hasler, 117-18
Takes refuge in Moors' cave, 132
Threatened with firing squad, 36-7
Threatens de Merode, 130-1
Training for 'Operation Frankton' (see separate entry)
Trains for Royal Marines, 3
Travels by train behind enemy lines, 103-4, 120-1, 126
Stewart, Captain Jock, 29
Stirling, C. L., 144
Stockport, 35
Stonehouse Barracks, 20
Swale, 39

Tannenfels, 73
Thames, 38, 39, 40
Tidal races, 52, 53
Training for 'Operation Frankton'
Assault course, 31
Bayonet drill, 31
Camouflaging the canoes, 43-4
Chichester harbour exercise, 30
Exercise code-named 'Blanket', 38-40
Limpet mines, 42-3
Training in Scotland, 40-4
Training in Southsea, 23-40
Swimming, 33, 40

Twelve chosen, 35
Underwater exercises, 40
Tirpitz, 15, 18, 43
Tripoli, 98

Victoria Cross, 143, 144
Villexavier, 80
Von Rundstedt, Field-Marshal Gerd, 58
Von Tippelskirch, Colonel, 58, 144

Wallace, Sergeant Samuel, 28, 31, 33, 36, 47, 51, 53, 57-8, 61, 64, 67, 72-3, 80, 143, 144, 146
Warlimont, General Walter, 58, 67
White Heather, 25, 27, 32, 142
Woodcock, Bruce, 122

Yorkshire, 25
'Young Belgian' (German agent), 127-30, 134, 136